Reading the
Bible
without
Getting Lost

Reading the Bible without Getting Lost

Mike Tune

LEAFWOOD
PUBLISHERS

READING THE BIBLE WITHOUT GETTING LOST

LEAFWOOD
PUBLISHERS

Copyright 2014 by Mike Tune

ISBN 978-0-89112-471-9
LCCN 2013042976

Printed in the United States of America

Scripture quotations, unless otherwise noted, are from The Holy Bible, New
International Version. Copyright 1984, International Bible Society. Used by permission
of Zondervan Publishers.

Library of Congress Cataloging-in-Publication Data
Tune, Mike.
  Reading the Bible without getting lost / Mike Tune.
      pages cm
  Includes bibliographical references and index.
  ISBN 978-0-89112-471-9 (alk. paper)
  1. Bible--Introductions. I. Title.
  BS475.3.T86 2011
  220.6'1--dc23
                                                                    2013042976

Cover design by Jennette Munger
Interior text design by Sandy Armstrong, Strong Design

Leafwood Publishers
1626 Campus Court
Abilene, Texas 79601
1-877-816-4455 toll free

For current information about all Leafwood titles, visit our website:
www.leafwoodpublishers.com

14 15 16 17 18 19 / 7 6 5 4 3 2 1

Contents

The Bible—
A "Book of Books"

For many Christians, the final authority for everything important about Christianity is the Bible. It is the only document thought to be from God.

The word "Bible" comes from a Greek word meaning "a little book." But the Bible is not just one book, and it is far from little.

The Bible is composed of 66 separate books.

It is divided into two sections. The first section is called the "Old Testament" and contains 39 books. The second section is called the "New Testament" and contains 27 books. These books were originally written in three languages. The books of the Old Testament were written in Hebrew and Aramaic. The books of the New Testament were written in Greek. They were all written over a period of 1500 years (from about 1400 BC to AD 100) by about 40 different authors. Some of these writers were political leaders. Others were religious leaders. Most were just ordinary people with a heart for God through whom God did extraordinary things.

The Story of the Bible

Though these forty men were separated by time and geography, the Bible tells just one story: God's great love for humankind and his determination to build a relationship with humanity.

The story begins with God creating all things, including the first man and woman. Though God gave the first man (Adam) and woman (Eve) everything necessary for a happy life, the Devil, God's enemy (also known as Satan), made them dissatisfied with their blessings and tempted them to disobey God. This disobedience is called "sin."

God is a perfect moral being, totally just, but all-loving and merciful. God could not overlook their sin, continue their fellowship, and be just. So from the moment humankind disobeyed, God set about creating a way to bring them back into fellowship with him. All of this happens in the first three chapters of the first Bible book, Genesis. From that point on, the story is about God's on-going effort to help people deal with their sins and live the kind of life God had in mind for them from the very beginning.

Testaments

God chose to work with humankind through agreements called "covenants." There are a number of these agreements mentioned in the Bible, but there are two main ones. The story of the first main covenant is found in the Old Testament. The story of the second covenant is found in the New Testament. One of the

Latin words for covenant is "testamentum." When the Bible was translated into Latin in the fourth century AD (called the "Vulgate" translation), the translator divided the books into "Old Testament" and "New Testament." Before that time, the Bible had no such divisions.

2

The Bible Story—
Old Testament

The Bible begins in Genesis with God, and his creation of all things—including humankind. God created humankind innocent and free from sin. But humankind became prideful, disobeyed God, and fell into sin. Repeatedly, God acted graciously, but humankind was determined not to listen to God, but to go their own way.

Like any parent, God was grieved that his children would turn their backs on him, and he sorrowed that they were determined to pursue courses of action that would only serve to hurt them. God tried a number of punishments to change their hearts, but ultimately, they all failed. This is the story of Genesis 1–11.

Not everyone turned against God, however. God decided to show humankind just how wonderful it would be to walk in fellowship with him. To make his point, and tell the story, he chose one man of faith and determined to work through his family as an object lesson to the world. That man's name was Abraham and he was from Mesopotamia, where Iraq is today. The next 38 chapters of Genesis tell the story of God guiding and blessing Abraham and his descendants—Isaac and Jacob. The story is not one of perfect people being blessed by God, but of imperfect people, struggling to walk with God, failing, and God guiding, helping, forgiving, and blessing them.

The story of Genesis ends about 1900 BC with God moving Abraham's descendants, the family of Jacob, to Egypt during a time of famine. He does this to save them from dying of starvation in their own land.

The Exodus

It's one thing for God to bless a family, another entirely to bless a whole nation of people. The book of Exodus takes up the story. For the next four hundred years, Jacob's family grows in Egypt until they number over a million. Because of their large number, the Egyptians felt threatened and enslaved them. God provides a leader, Moses, who leads this large nation out of Egypt to a land God had promised to Abraham. This land we know as Israel or Palestine. The journey to that land is known as the Exodus, and is covered in Exodus, Leviticus, Numbers, and Deuteronomy. The first five books of the Bible were written by Moses and are called the Pentateuch (meaning "five books"). On the way to that land, God met with this people at a mountain called Sinai and gave them his laws. The account of these laws is also covered in the Pentateuch (Exodus 19–Numbers 10:10). Once again, despite all God did for his people, they found walking with God a continual struggle. It was a choice between living God's way and living their own way. All too often, living their own way won out. This struggle was signified by the fact that God's people became known as Israel, another name for Jacob meaning "struggles with God." Deuteronomy ends about 1400 BC.

Settlement

Before Israel arrived in their new home, Moses died and God appointed a new leader, Joshua. The story of their entry into their promised land is recounted in the book of Joshua.

For the next 400 years, Israel settled and spread out in the land of Canaan, but they still struggled with God. They would turn from God. God would discipline them. They would turn to God, and God would rescue and bless them. The story is repeated over and over again in the book of Judges, named for the rulers of Israel during this time. Not all is dark, however. The story of Ruth provides a wonderful interlude to assure us that there were good people during that time.

The reason for Israel's great struggle with God was that she wanted to be like the people around her rather than be like God wanted her to be. This point is made in the book of Samuel where Israel asks for a king so that she can be like the other nations. God wanted to be her king, but Israel refused.

Kingdom—United, Divided, Exiled, and Restored

The first king of Israel was a man named Saul. His story is found in 1 Samuel 8–31. Saul was followed by David whose story is found in 2 Samuel, in 1 Kings 1:1–2:12, and in 1 Chronicles 11–29. David was also a poet and the book of Psalms is attributed to him. David was followed by his son Solomon and his reign is recounted in 1 Kings 2–11 and 2 Chronicles 1–9. Solomon wrote the books of Ecclesiastes, Proverbs, and the Song of Solomon.

At Solomon's death, the people of God divided into two nations: a northern nation which retained the name Israel and a southern nation called Judah.

Over the next 200 years, the northern nation determined once and for all to abandon fellowship with God. God sent a number of messengers (called "prophets") to her during this time. They all have books of the Bible associated with their names and are as follows: Isaiah, Hosea, Amos, and Jonah.

God also sent prophets to the southern kingdom during the same time period, including Isaiah and Joel. By 722 BC, God had worked with Israel long enough and determined to destroy her as a nation, never to rise again. He did that by leading the Assyrian armies against her and having her carried captive to foreign lands. The period between 900 and 722 BC is covered in 1 Kings 12–17 and 2 Chronicles 10–28.

The southern kingdom continued until 586 BC. She too continued to struggle with God and the Lord sent to her prophets like Jeremiah (who also wrote Lamentations), Micah, and Habakkuk. The account of the southern kingdom is told in 2 Chronicles 29–36 and 2 Kings 18–25.

Finally, the southern kingdom's rebellion against God could be tolerated no more. In 586 BC, God sent the Babylonian army against her and destroyed the nation, her capital city of Jerusalem, and even the temple of the Lord. Judah had thought that the presence of the temple would save them without having to live holy lives. She was wrong. For the next 70 years, she suffered captivity in the land of Babylon. During this time, God continued to address his people through Daniel and Ezekiel.

It's a long story and you might well wonder why it is important. But this story illustrates the tendency of humankind to go its own way rather than God's way. It further illustrates God's great attachment to his chosen people, his unwillingness to give her up, his determination that she live the life he designed for her, and his willingness to forgive and restore. To his people God said: "Can a mother forget the baby at her breast and have no compassion on the child she has borne? Though she may forget, I will not forget you! See, I have engraved you on the palms of my hands; your walls are ever before me" (Isaiah 49:15–16).

In 539 BC, after a difficult exile, God's people were allowed to go home (read the story in Ezra and Nehemiah) as God had promised. Though not without some reluctance and continued struggle, they rebuilt the city of Jerusalem and its temple, and for the next several years God continued to speak to them through prophets like Haggai, Zechariah, and Malachi.

The Old Testament focuses on one family, the descendants of Abraham. God does it to illustrate how great a God he is, how kind, benevolent, insistent, and loving he can be. And throughout the story, God speaks of a day when the invitation to be his people will be extended, not just to one family, but to the whole world. The fulfillment of that promise will take place in the New Testament story.

3

The Bible Story—
New Testament

It was always God's intent that all races, nations, and peoples
have an opportunity to come to know him and become his
people. You can see this in a variety of texts throughout the Old
Testament, but these three from Zechariah and Malachi stand
out:

- "Many nations will be joined with the LORD in that
  day and will become my people. I will live among you
  and you will know that the LORD Almighty has sent
  me to you." (Zechariah 2:11).
- "And many peoples and powerful nations will come
  to Jerusalem to seek the LORD Almighty and to
  entreat him. This is what the LORD Almighty says:
  'In those days ten men from all languages and nations
  will take firm hold of one Jew by the hem of his robe

and say, `Let us go with you, because we have heard that God is with you.'" (Zechariah 8:22–23).

- "'My name will be great among the nations, from the rising to the setting of the sun. In every place incense and pure offerings will be brought to my name, because my name will be great among the nations,' says the LORD Almighty" (Malachi 1:11).

The problem, of course, was that in the time of the Old Testament, there was no way for anyone to become one of God's people who was not born a descendant of Abraham. While it was possible for Gentiles to attach themselves to God's people as "converts" and participate in the festivals, they were not actually Jews. In this way, God emphasized that belonging to him was a matter of God's initiative, not humanity's.

But God had a plan. One day, anyone who wanted to could become one of his people. Anyone considering that though would need to know what being one of God's people was all about. They would need to know why that status was important. They would also need to know what God expected of them.

The Old Testament provides that information. But it remained for Jesus to come and make the actual adoption process possible.

The **New Testament** begins with the birth of Jesus. God himself became human, born in a natural way. He did it to show that a human could live a holy life. He also did it to demonstrate the full extent of God's love. None of the Gospel accounts (Matthew, Mark, Luke, and John) were written to provide a biography of Jesus, but all of them contain biographical information and cover the time period from about 4 BC to 30 AD.

To all who would entrust their lives to the leading of Jesus, his death paid the price for their sins and opened the door for them to become God's people.

The book of Acts of the Apostles tells how that message spread, from 30 AD to about 62 AD. It also tells us how the message of Jesus changed people's lives.

In Acts we are introduced to an exceptional figure in Saul of Tarsus. Saul was a devout Jew, well-educated and a part of the Jerusalem aristocracy. His becoming a Christian is a bold statement in the book of Acts that no longer is anyone a person of God because of heritage. Being a person of God requires one to turn to God through faith in Jesus. The conversion of Saul is recounted in Acts three times to make that point very plain. No one becomes part of God's people because they live a good life or because they are well connected. Surrender to Jesus is paramount.

Saul became a missionary. Acts recounts three mission trips. During the second one (48–54 AD—Acts 15–18), Paul wrote his letters to the Galatians and the Thessalonians. During the third journey (55–57 AD—Acts 19–21) he wrote at least two letters to the Corinthians and the one to the Romans. The message of the gospel caused trouble wherever it went—mainly because no one wanted to believe they were not already God's people (especially the Jews), and particularly because it required submission to Jesus, who had been crucified (the most degrading of all capital punishments). Christian missionaries (including Saul, who came to be known as Paul) felt this opposition often and suffered immensely for it.

In 58 AD, Paul was arrested in Jerusalem. Because he was both a Jew and a Roman citizen, he appealed his case to Caesar and in 60 AD he was taken to Rome for trial (Acts 22–28). He remained there for two years, during which time he wrote the letters to Philemon, the Ephesians, the Philippians, and the Colossians.

There, the historical presentation of the book of Acts ends (62 AD). From what we can piece together, Paul was acquitted by the Roman court and released. During the next six years (62–68 AD), he would travel extensively and write his letters to Timothy and Titus. All the letters contained in the New Testament were written to Christians struggling with their faith, trying to live holy lives in a "crooked and depraved generation" (Philippians 2:15). The letters were written to guide and direct the Christian reader in holiness.

Between 62 and 68 AD, Peter, a disciple of Jesus while he was on the earth, wrote both the letters that bear his name. A short time after the martyrdom of Peter and Paul, the letter to the Hebrews was written, as were the letters written by Jesus' earthly brothers, James and Jude.

The last apostle to die was John; he wrote, sometime near the end of the first century, three letters which bear his name, his Gospel account, and the book of Revelation. By the end of the first century AD, the New Testament was complete.

4

The Literature of the Bible

Our newspapers contain different types of literature. News items are written differently from editorials. Neither is anything like the comics. You shouldn't read the comics the way you read the news. The same principle applies to the Bible. You shouldn't read the Psalms the same way you read the Gospel of Matthew. They are different types of biblical literature.

Historical narrative in the Bible tells a story to make a point. This literature contains history, but is not written to be history. The book of Acts is "historical narrative." It is not a history book, for there is much Acts leaves out. Rather, it is a book that contains history organized to make a point. Your task as a reader is to determine what point the writer was making. Sometimes the writer himself will tell you. John, for example, in his Gospel, writes at the end: "Jesus did many other miraculous signs in the presence of his disciples, which are not recorded in this book. But these are written that you may believe that Jesus is the Christ, the Son of God, and that by believing you may have life in his name" (John 20:30–31). Here John tells you that his book concentrates on the miraculous signs Jesus did. They are a focal point. Those miracle stories John told were to convince the reader that Jesus was the Son of God and cause the reader to put his trust in Jesus. The result would be a better life—an eternal life.

In the beginning of Luke's Gospel he wrote: "since I myself have carefully investigated everything from the beginning, it seemed good also to me to write an orderly account for you . . . so that you may know the certainty of the things you have been taught" (Luke 1:4). Most students get so caught up in making application of Luke's Gospel and Acts that they forget why he wrote those books: to show the certainty of Christianity.

Books of historical narrative are Genesis, Numbers, Joshua-Esther, Job, and Matthew-Acts.

Poetry is another type of biblical literature. Poetry expresses the deep emotion of the heart. Sometimes it is deliberately instructive. At other times it tells a story. But at all times poetry tends to exaggerate because it is heart-felt rather than coldly logical and calculatingly exact. You have to be careful interpreting poetry. In Psalm 51, David wrote: "Surely I was sinful at birth, sinful from the time my mother conceived me." Some interpreters, forgetting this is poetry, have treated it as if it were one of Paul's letters or part of a law code. They have surmised that David was saying that babies are born sinful or have inherited the sins of their parents or forefathers. But when you see that the poem was written just after David had been identified as an adulterer by the prophet Nathan, and when you read of his anguish and guilt, you understand that David was simply saying: "I've been a sinner all my life."

In Psalm 109:8–11 David writes:

May his days be few;
may another take his place of leadership.
May his children be fatherless
and his wife a widow.
May his children be wandering beggars;
may they be driven from their ruined homes.
May a creditor seize all he has;
may strangers plunder the fruits of his labor.

What a horrible sentiment! Yet this is not what David is asking God to do, but what David's accusers are saying about him! David does turn around and ask the Lord to do to his accusers what they are doing to him, but this is not a license to mistreat people. Most recently I saw this passage cited on a bumper sticker referring to our president. Because they got it from the Bible, I assume that the creators of the bumper sticker thought the sentiment appropriate; yet David refers to those who say such things as "wicked and deceitful men."

Sometimes people so mistreat you that you want to get back at them. But if we get any lesson from this passage it ought to be that when you feel vengeful "take your thoughts to God in prayer."

Proverbs 22:6 says, "Train a child in the way he should go, and when he is old he will not turn from it." Often this piece of poetry has been read as a guarantee, like a law of promise. If you raise your children right, they'll turn out right. Conversely, if they didn't turn out right, it's the parents' fault. Because the proverbs are poetry, they should be read as advice for living, not as guarantees. The best way to raise children is God's way. If you don't raise them that way, they probably won't go God's way. But even if you do, it's not a guarantee they will stick with the Lord. The books of poetry are Psalms, Proverbs, Ecclesiastes, and the Song of Solomon.

A third type of biblical literature we might call "sermons." We could call these books "prophecy," but we won't for a very good reason: prophecy, in the minds of most people, means fore-telling the future. While it is true that books of prophecy do sometimes mention events yet to come, that is a minor reason for their existence. When books of prophecy are read just for their future-telling, students miss the most important parts of the books. Some Bible students look at the prophets only for what they say about Jesus. But few of them say much at all about Jesus. These books were written mainly to call sinners to repentance and obedience to the will of God. As such, they resemble sermons. The future prophecies they contain usually have to do with the punishment God is sending because of the readers' dis-obedience. These sermons of the prophets help us to understand better what is important to God. The sermon books are Isaiah through Malachi in the Old Testament.

Another form of biblical literature is legal writings. You will find legal literature in sections of Exodus, Leviticus, Numbers, and Deuteronomy (though Deuteronomy contains mostly ser-mons calling the people to remember and keep the laws of God). There are nearly 600 different commands in the Old Testament, and all of them are found in the first five books of the Bible. Some of these laws are civil, applying to the government of Israel in the land of Canaan. Other laws apply to Israel's ritual worship of God. These rituals were keyed to Israel's experiences with God and were not intended for non-Jewish observance. Ethical laws regulate the moral behavior of God's people and these are the laws most often emphasized in the New Testament.

Letters, also called epistles, are another form of biblical literature. They are found only in the New Testament. These letters are written to individuals or churches to address specific concerns of God—specifically that they cease improper behavior. To interpret these letters correctly, you must determine from the letter itself the situation of the readers and how the writer wants the readers to respond.

A final type of literature in the Bible is often called "apocalyptic"—a special type of drama that is foreign to us today. It is found in the book of Revelation and to some measure in Daniel, Zechariah, Ezekiel, and Matthew. The writers use all kinds of images to get the attention of the reader and to dramatize the message in a memorable way.

For example, Ezekiel uses an image of a wheel within a wheel (chapter 1). Just trying to imagine that image can be frustratingly difficult, but Ezekiel tells us that this image represents the presence of God (1:28), the glory of the Lord. Later in the book, the image is picked up again. Idolatry is going on in the Jerusalem temple. The wheel within the wheel rises and moves to the door of the temple, then to the east gate (chapter 10). Finally the image departs Jerusalem altogether (chapter 11). The point, well dramatized in the text, is that God's presence has departed from the temple and Jerusalem.

Not every image in apocalyptic literature will have meaning. Sometimes it is there just as color. If the image has particular significance, the writer will explain it.

The word "apocalyptic" does not occur in the Bible. It is a derivation of a Greek word which means "to reveal." Keep in mind that the purpose of this kind of literature is not to hide the truth, but to reveal it. The writer is painting a picture of what is going on in the lives of the characters involved (or what will go on), and calling them to a specific way of life, God's way. It doesn't hurt to think of this literature as a type of ancient "Star Wars" movie—as long as you remember that this is not a movie or a play, but the Word of God.

These are the types of literature in the Bible. Each one needs to be approached differently in order to get the point the author, moved by God, intended.

5

How to Study the Bible

The following are steps to better Bible study.

Step 1—Read the Bible. Read it *regularly*. A daily reading of scripture breaks down a seemingly daunting task into something manageable. There are a number of daily Bible reading schedules available that will, by reading as little as three and a half chapters a day, get you through the Bible in a year.

Read the Bible *thoroughly*. *All* scripture is inspired of God and being familiar with *all* of it is necessary for understanding God, his way, his thinking, and his people.

Step 2—Be familiar with the different types of literature. Each type is approached differently.

Step 3—Ask questions about the book itself or the section of Scripture:

1) What can we determine about the writer?

2) What can we determine about the first readers?

3) How is the book structured?

4) What was the book's message to its first readers?

5) Only after asking and answering these questions will you be able to answer the final and most important question: How does this book's message apply to me? A book of the Bible has no different message for us than it did the first readers. We must determine the original message first.

To help see how this works, I am going to take a book from each of the different types of biblical literature and answer these questions from the book itself. We will look first at a "letter" in the New Testament. Our sample will be Paul's letter to the Philippians.

Studying Letters

I will use two reference aids in our study. The first is a comparative translation. Always read at least two translations of the Bible in your study. Translations are geared to reading levels just like newspapers, which are written at a sixth-grade reading level or below. The New International Version is prepared at an eighth-grade reading level; the Good News Bible at a sixth-grade level; the New Century Bible at a third-grade level. Whatever Bible you usually use, select an easier reading version for comparison.

The second help is a good Bible dictionary. There are several one-volume editions and some large multi-volume ones. Buy the biggest and newest you can afford. Old Bible dictionaries are like old encyclopedias—not always the best source.

STOP: Before reading any further, read Philippians for yourself.

1) What can we determine about the writer?

We know that his name was Paul and he was in the company of a man named Timothy (1:1). We also know that he was in chains (1:13, 14), probably meaning prison. He refers to the "palace guard" in 1:13. Looking at a different translation, we see that this is also called the "praetorian guard." A Bible dictionary reveals this to be an elite guard stationed in Rome. So we know that Paul was in prison in Rome when he wrote this book.

Paul seems to have some concern about his own future. He writes: "I eagerly expect and hope that I . . . will have sufficient courage so that Christ will be exalted . . . whether by my life or by death" (1:20).

2) What can we determine about the first readers?

We can know the first readers were Christians living in the city of Philippi. Looking up Philippi in a Bible dictionary, we discover the city was located in the northern part of Greece and that Paul went there the first time on his second missionary journey. We are told that the story of that journey is found in Acts 16 (if you are not familiar with that story, read it to help you understand Paul's relationship with these people). The church in Philippi is well organized because they have both "overseers" and "deacons" (1:1).

They were enduring some persecution themselves. Paul wrote, "For it has been granted to you on behalf of Christ not only to believe on him, but also to suffer for him, since you are going through the same struggle you saw I had, and now hear that I still have" (1:29–30). Referring back to Acts 16, Paul was unjustly imprisoned in Philippi back then, and he is also unjustly imprisoned when he writes this book.

In chapter three Paul mentions in a condemning way a group of people who have "confidence in the flesh." Paul helps us understand what this means in the following verses. He says that if anyone has the right to put "confidence in the flesh" he (Paul) surely would. His family line was special (descendant of the tribe of Benjamin), his nationality was special (an Israelite), his parentage was special (both were Hebrews), his religion was special (he was a Pharisee), and his devotion to God was special (faultless) (3:4–6). As a beginning Bible student you may not understand the significance of all these things, but you cannot fail to miss the fact that they all have to do with status. And so, "confidence in the flesh" has to do with being "stuck on yourself" because of who you are. These people were troublemakers among the Philippian believers.

In chapter four we discover two Christian women in the Philippian church are having difficulty getting along. These women were partners in Paul's ministry. They had "contended at Paul's side in the cause of the gospel." This is no minor spat and Paul urges the church to help them solve their differences and be involved in healing the breach between them (4:2–3).

3) What is the book's message and how does it deliver that message?

Three situations present themselves in the church at Philippi. First, the church is facing persecution. Second, the church is troubled by some who thought they were better than others because of their status. Third, there was division between two personalities serious enough to involve the whole church.

When Paul begins the letter, the first thing he writes is how much he loves these Christians and how confident he is God is moving among them (1:3–6). He assures them, some of whom are in prison as he is, that his imprisonment has actually advanced the cause of Jesus. Some, seeing Paul's plight, have taken courage and spoken the word of God boldly (1:14). Even Paul's guards have come to know Jesus (1:13) and Paul says he intends to live so that, no matter what happens, live or die, Jesus will be exalted (1:20).

To Christians struggling with worldly status (remember that "confidence in the flesh"?), Paul cites his own example as a person who counted the highest status in his nation but garbage (3:8) that he might know Christ and receive his blessings. Near the end of that discussion, Paul writes that "all of us who are mature should take such a view of things" (3:15).

To people who are having trouble getting along with each other, Paul presents three examples of selfless sacrifice (chapter 2). First, Christ, who though God, made himself nothing and sacrificed himself so God might be glorified (2:6–11). Second, Timothy, who is coming to them shortly and who, Paul says, always looks after the interests of others before his own (2:21). And third, Epaphroditus, who risked his own life to help Paul (2:25–27).

With those lessons in mind, Paul ends the book with an order to "get along" with one another and take every problem to God in prayer, believing God will hear them and take care of them (chapter 4)

4) How does this book's message apply to me?

Philippians tells me that whatever happens in my life, I should face all situations with the determination to bring honor to God. It tells me that to follow in the footsteps of great people of faith, and especially the footsteps of Jesus, I should be willing to give up whatever it takes for the good of others (put others first). And last but not least, Philippians tells me that I should talk to God about my life, trusting him to help make it what he wants it to be.

NOTE: If you are an experienced Bible student, you may wonder why I have not pointed the student to more Bible helps. Commentaries, for example, tell about the background to a book and discuss in detail each verse. But frankly, that's cheating. If you go to the commentary before you ask and answer these questions, you will not be studying the Bible. You will be studying a person's commentary on the Word of God rather than the Word of God itself. You may end up knowing more commentary than Bible.

Studying Poetry

Psalms, Proverbs, Ecclesiastes, Song of Solomon, and even Job are usually considered the poetry books. But poetry is found elsewhere in the Bible. Most of the book of Isaiah is written in poetic form. There are poetic passages in the New Testament; Philippians 2:6–11, 1 Timothy 3:16, and 2 Timothy 2:11–13 are examples of poetry found there. For this study, however, we will examine poetry in the Old Testament.

Old Testament poetry can be divided into two parts: that which looks like poetry, and that which sounds like advice. The "advice" poetry is sometimes called "wisdom" literature and is mainly comprised of Proverbs and Ecclesiastes. Most simply, it is the purpose of wisdom to give advice in applying the law of God to daily living and we will look at this kind of poetry first.

It is true that the Old Testament law prohibited adultery. Wisdom literature however takes that a step further and warns against keeping company with those who are inclined to be sexually immoral (Proverbs 5:1–6). To those who would read the adultery law literally and insist that only "going all the way" is forbidden, wisdom literature reveals that all sexual activity is forbidden unless it is with your marriage partner (Proverbs 5:15–20).

The Law demanded obedience to parents. Wisdom literature goes beyond that to advise "listening" to the advice of parents so that life will be all God wants it to be. The advice parents give should be so dear to you that you are willing to pay any price to hear it (see Proverbs 4:3–7). Of course, that also means parents should make sure their advice is good and not just poorly considered prejudice.

Since it is poetry, wisdom literature is very graphic. When discussing sexual activity the writer says, "Should your springs overflow in the streets, your streams of water in the public squares? Let them be yours alone, never to be shared with strangers. May your fountain be blessed, and may you rejoice in the wife of your youth" (Proverbs 5:16–18). In a society where everyone understood the precious value of water in a desert, to describe sexuality in terms of water makes it most precious indeed, not to be wasted or misused.

Poetry should not be read as "law." It does not offer guarantees. It simply offers the kind of good advice a parent would give a child—though, in the case of poetry in the Bible, it is advice from God.

Poetry should be read as a unit. All that the book of Proverbs has to say on a subject should be considered before any one piece of advice is followed. The same is true of Ecclesiastes.

Ecclesiastes seems like a depressing book. Repeatedly (38 times to be exact) the author refers to the meaningless nature of life. But only when you read the book carefully and completely is this very cynical view placed in proper perspective. Ecclesiastes also uses another phrase: "under the sun." It occurs 27 times.

The point of the book is that when life is viewed only from an earthly perspective ("under the sun"), it easily becomes meaningless and one's outlook cynical. But when you look beyond the sun to God (that's the last chapter), life can be greatly rewarding.

One final point: because this is poetry, it is important to read it in a translation with which you are comfortable. Poetry can be difficult enough to read without getting lost in archaic jargon.

We turn now to poetry that "looks like poetry" rather than "sounds like advice."

The Psalms comprise the largest single body of literature in the Old Testament and it's easy to get lost in them. But with this poetry, I find it most helpful to take each chapter as a unit and ask the following questions:

1) What is the situation of the writer?
2) How might I feel in this situation?
3) How does the writer say he feels?
4) What message is the writer trying to convey?

Sometimes, a psalm will not contain all the answers to these questions. Psalm 23 answers only the last two, but others are more informative.

Read psalm 25 before going further.

The writer of this psalm is David. We see that in the heading. Some people don't think those headings were originally a part of Psalms, but we have no manuscripts of Psalms without them. Generally, unless there is good reason to believe otherwise, the heading is trustworthy and can be a great source of information. For example, the heading in psalm 51 tells you that it was written after David had committed adultery. Psalm 59 was written when David was on the run from King Saul.

In psalm 25, David tells us that he feels alone. The only company he feels is the hot pursuit of his enemies who "fiercely" hate him and seek to take his life.

If I were in that position, I would be wondering "Where are you, Lord?"

But in the psalm David reminds himself God has promised that no one who puts their trust in God will be put to shame. He calls on God to remember that promise. He reminds God that God's own integrity is on the line (verses 20–21). And in the psalm, David insists that he is coming to God because he has placed his trust in the Lord. He knows no one else can deliver him (verse 15).

So what is the message for us?

First, it is most important to live a life that demonstrates your trust in God. You can say it all you want, but if your life does not show it, the trust isn't there.

Second, when the trust is there, you can call on God to be faithful to his promises to help you—even to keep you from being embarrassed!

Third, your relationship with God ought to be so close that you find yourself going to God often, sharing with him your every joy and problem. Of course, I didn't get this from psalm 25 only, but from all of them! Why was David a "man after God's own heart" (Acts 13:22)? Because God was his friend and confidant and you can see it in the way David wrote and in the number of prayers he penned.

Other Psalms present special problems. Psalm 3:7 and 58:6 call on God to break the teeth of the author's enemies. Is that something we should pray today?

Christians are going to have enemies. Those enemies will provoke us to anger. There may be times we will feel like hitting someone. But what these and other psalms say is that we should not beat ourselves up because we have those feelings. Rather, we should take those feelings to God and leave the punishment of our enemies to him. We may want to break their teeth, but whether they are actually broken should be left in God's hands.

When we can do that, we will find ourselves dependent on God, and that's what faith is really all about.

Studying the Prophets
STOP: Before reading any further, read Amos for yourself.

1) What can we know about the writer?

In the first verse of his book, Amos tells us he was a shepherd from the city of Tekoa. He also says he lived and worked as a prophet during the reigns of Uzziah, King of Judah, and Jeroboam, son of Jehoash, King of Israel.

David's son, Solomon, was the third king of God's people. When he died, the empire was split into two kingdoms, north and south. The north was called Israel and the south Judah. The two kingdoms existed, with their own kings and governments, until the Northern Kingdom was destroyed by the Assyrians in 722 BC. Amos dates himself during the last years of this divided nation. Uzziah ruled from 790 to 740 BC and Jeroboam ruled from 793 to 752 BC.

Tekoa, where Amos was from, was in the southern kingdom of Judah, about 15 miles south of Jerusalem. Though Amos was from the south, his message was for the Northern Kingdom, Israel. Thus God gave his servant the task of going to a place where he was considered a spy and a traitor, and delivering a less than welcome message.

Amos was neither a priest nor a trained prophet. He was not educated for the work God entrusted to his care. He was a shepherd and a part-time gardener (Amos 7:14). But God called him to be his spokesman.

2) What can we know about the first readers?

Amos opens with a message for a variety of nations. He addresses Syria (referred to as Damascus, her capital city), Philistia (Gaza was her capital city), Phoenicia (Tyre), Edom, Ammon, Moab, and Judah. He reserved his main message, however, for Israel.

Israel was guilty of terrible human rights abuses. Her people oppress the poor terribly and force slave girls into horrible sexual abuses (2:6–7). Israel has become rich, and her concentration on materialism shows with the proliferation of winter and summer homes decorated with ivory (3:15). The wealthy women spend their time in luxury and drunkenness. In fact, it would seem that prosperity has been Israel's downfall. She has a tremendous army (5:3) and estates with new stone mansions and gardens (5:11). In and of itself, there would be nothing wrong with wealth. But the problem had to do with the way Israel became wealthy, and what it has done to her relationship with God.

Israel has become wealthy through "skimping the measure, boosting the price, and cheating with dishonest scales" (8:5–6). She has used her wealth to abuse poor people and increase their poverty (2:7; 4:1; 5:11–12; 8:4,6). She has tried to cover up her cruelty and materialism by being "religious." In fact, the more religion the better. Not only does she give to God, but also to idols. "'Go to Bethel and sin; go to Gilgal and sin yet more. Bring your sacrifices every morning, your tithes every three years. Burn leavened bread as a thank offering and brag about your freewill offerings—boast about them, you Israelites, for this is what you love to do,' declares the Sovereign LORD" (Amos 4:4–5). Even if you don't understand all the implications of these verses, you get the picture that Israel was very religious, but in an unacceptable way. They were what we would call "good church-goin' folks," but they had no heart for God.

In fact, sometimes their "church-going" got in the way of making money, which caused them to regret they were so religious. Amos cried: "Hear this, you who trample the needy and do away with the poor of the land, saying, 'When will the New Moon be over that we may sell grain, and the Sabbath be ended that we may market wheat?'" (8:4–5). They can't wait for the religious festivals to be over so they can get back to business.

3) What was the book's message to its first readers?

You might expect God, through the prophet, to condemn these practices. But there is more than that in Amos. Evidently God has "had it" with their sinfulness because in Amos he pronounces certain doom. Fifty-six times in 115 verses, God announces what he will do:

- "I will not turn back my wrath" (1:3, 6, 9, 11, 13; 2:1, 4, 6).
- "I will destroy the king" (1:5).
- "I will crush you as a cart crushes when loaded with grain" (2:13).
- "I will deliver up the city and everything in it" (6:8).
- "I will spare them no longer" (7:8).
- "I will make the sun go down at noon and darken the earth in broad daylight. I will turn your religious feasts into mourning and all your singing into weeping. I will make all of you wear sackcloth and shave

your heads. I will make that time like mourning for an
only son and the end of it like a bitter day" (8:9–10).

- "They will fall never to rise again" (8:14).

There will be no escape. "The swift will not escape, the
strong will not muster their strength, and the warrior will not
save his life. The archer will not stand his ground, the fleet-
footed soldier will not get away, and the horseman will not save
his life" (2:14–15). "It will be as though a man fled from a lion
only to meet a bear, as though he entered his house and rested
his hand on the wall only to have a snake bite him" (5:19).

Sometimes in the prophetic writings, an announced doom
may be conditional. God will say, "Unless you turn to me, I will
punish you." But by Amos' day, time for repentance was over.
God promised to send the people of the Northern Kingdom into
exile where they would be a nation no more. This happened
in 722 BC when the Assyrian army of Sargon II marched on
Samaria and deported the inhabitants of the land.

God assures us through the prophet that he has given the
people ample warning. In 4:6–12 he says: "I gave you empty
stomachs in every city and lack of bread in every town, . . . I also
withheld rain from you when the harvest was still three months
away. . . . I sent plagues among you as I did to Egypt. I killed your
young men with the sword . . ." Though God did all these things,
Israel still refused to return to him. And so, because Israel was
impenitent, the Lord said: "prepare to meet your God," a pro-
nouncement of doom.

Earlier I mentioned that Amos began with a condemnation of
other nations. He described the nations' sins. Interestingly, their
sins were very much like the sins of Israel. God is saying Israel
has become like the other nations. She can expect the same fate.

4) How does this book's message apply to me?

First, whether the world knows him or not, the Lord is God of the world. He holds the world accountable for knowing him and acting with decency before him. Not having a covenant with God is no excuse. Whether you know God or not, you will be accountable to him.

God has a particular interest in his own people knowing him and acting accordingly. When his people become so attached to the world that God becomes secondary—or even an inconvenience—God will act to get their attention. God may send trouble or distress on them. He may even take their lives. God wants them to yield to his will. Ultimately, if they do not, he will destroy them. No one, not even the people of God, can rebel with impunity before the one who made Pleiades and Orion, who calls forth the waters of the sea and pours them out over the face of the land, the one who brings even the most fortified nation to ruin (Amos 5:7–10).

These messages still apply. No, God is not threatening to send rebellious people "beyond Damascus." But he does intend to be active in the lives of his people, disciplining them, and taking whatever action is necessary. In a nation like our own, so given to religion and materialism, Amos is a prophet we need to hear often.

Studying Historical Narrative

Genesis, Joshua, Judges, Ruth, Samuel, Kings, Chronicles, and Matthew through Acts are all examples of literature called "historical narrative." This literature tells a true story, but its point is not just to tell a story. The story is presented to make a specific point. Sometimes, the author will plainly state the point he wishes to make.

After recounting a number of miracles (most of them only found in John's Gospel), John wrote: "Jesus did many other miraculous signs in the presence of his disciples, which are not recorded in this book. But these are written that you may believe that Jesus is the Christ, the Son of God, and that by believing you may have life in his name." John's focus was to get people to trust Jesus. In doing that, he believed their lives would be changed for the better.

Because of John's specifically stated purpose, you should read his Gospel account asking these specific questions:

- What does each miracle tell you about Jesus that would cause you to trust him?
- What does Jesus' life and teaching tell you about the kind of life God wants you to have?

In the first miracle story, John tells of Jesus' turning water to wine. The Lord was a guest at a wedding feast when the hosts ran out of wine. This, of course, would be an embarrassment to the hosts, and Jesus' mother asked him to do something about it. Jesus does, making the very best wine from water. The miracle makes several points: First, Jesus has power over matter. He can change one substance into another with no trouble at all. Second, Jesus is willing to use that power to save his friends from embarrassment.

Could you trust a fellow like that? Sure.

And each time John tells a miracle story, he is making a similar point.

In John's account, he refers to "life" about 50 times. Seventeen of those times he connects "life" with the word "eternal." In our culture, eternal life means you live forever. But when you think about it, everyone is going to live forever. Some will live forever in heaven, others in hell. So what's so special about "eternal life"? "Eternal life" doesn't refer to the length of time you live, but rather to the quality of life you enjoy. In the Bible "eternal life" is the best life, the one God wants believers to enjoy.

What does turning the water to wine tell you about the eternal life? It says simply that Jesus is able to take care of all of life's difficulties. Those who ask him can expect him to act in their best interest according to the will of God. That being true, why should we worry?

Not all historical narratives specifically state the author's purpose. When that happens, we have to ask: what keeps coming up most often in this story?

In Judges we notice a repeated rise and fall in the story among God's people. When there is no moral leader among the people, they digress into sin. When God raises up a moral leader, the people change their lives and turn to God. As we get near the end of the book, a phrase occurs which is repeated four times: "There was no king in Israel" (17:6; 18:1; 19:1; 21:25). Two of those times, the author adds "everyone did as he saw fit."

Here is the point of the book: When people look to themselves for their own guidance and authority, they will eventually become morally bankrupt. They need an authority to submit to. But they must make sure the authority they submit to is worthy of their obedience, and the only way to do that is to measure one's life by the Word of God.

God has not left us on our own to live as we please. We must be a submissive people, and submissive supremely to God. We must actively seek guidance, and that guidance must come from God.

Luke and Acts are two historical narratives written by the same author. Together, they comprise the largest single part of the New Testament. Luke, insisting he had carefully researched everything from the very beginning, says the purpose of his books is so his readers might know the "certainty" of the things they had been taught. As you read through Luke's Gospel, you will want to ask two questions: First, what is the evidence Luke cites to prove the trustworthiness of the Christian story? Second, what is the substance of the Christian message Luke seeks to prove?

Luke insists that the deeds done by Jesus and his disciples were sufficient to support their claims to have the authority of God. When confronted by spiritual forces of immense strength and reputation, Jesus and his disciples are always seen to be superior to those forces. Jesus is able to cast out a legion of demons (Luke 8:30). The power of the disciples is shown to be superior to that of famous people who are regarded as gods (read the account of Simon the sorcerer in Acts 8) and at times they are regarded as gods themselves (Acts 14:11–13). God works "extraordinary" miracles through Paul so that "even handkerchiefs and aprons that had touched him were taken to the sick, and their illnesses were cured and the evil spirits left them."

The skeptic of Luke's day would wonder if these stories were really true. Luke assures his readers they are. He notes that these events did not take place behind closed doors (Acts 26:26). Fifteen times in his books he says the events "amazed" the people. Thirty-five times he notes that "crowds" of people saw them. The fame of Jesus spread throughout the countryside (Luke 4:14, 37; 7:17) and people from every village in Galilee and Judea came to hear him (Luke 5:17). Even the opponents of Christianity confessed that his disciples had "filled Jerusalem" with their teaching (Acts 5:28) and the message of Christ was known "everywhere" (Acts 28:20–22). At times, Jesus and his disciples were almost crushed by the crowds (Luke 8:42). The whole point of this material in Luke's story is to convince the reader that everyone knew the truthfulness of the story and that there are sufficient witnesses to verify the events and the teaching.

Luke even made it easy for his first readers to check out the story by giving names and addresses of the people involved and the list reads like a Who's Who list in the ancient world.

Some would be favorable to Christianity:

Zaccheus, the wealthy chief tax-collector in Jericho
Manaen (a preacher in Antioch who had been raised with King Herod -- Acts 13:1)
Jarius (a synagogue ruler in Galilee)
Joanna, the wife of Herod's second in command
Simon, a tanner in Joppa
Sergius Paulus, the proconsul who ruled the senatorial province of Cyprus

Others would not be so favorable:

Annas, Caiphas, John and Alexander, Gamaliel and Sosthenes, all Jewish leaders
Gallio, the governor of Asia
Pilate, Felix, and Festus, governors of Judea
Demetrius, a silversmith in Ephesus

By giving these names and a host of others, most of whom could be easily located in the time of Luke, the author invites his readers to "check out the story" and verify, as he had done, its truthfulness.

What had Luke's first readers been taught? To get an answer, you have to take note of the things in Luke and Acts that are repeatedly mentioned. One example is the innocence of Christianity. Romans saw all new religions as enemies of the Roman social order. Christianity did fine as long as it was perceived as a sect of Judaism. But when it was recognized that Christianity was not Judaism, there was trouble. It is significant that, near the end of Luke, Jesus is pronounced "innocent" of any crime three times (Luke 23:4, 15, 22). Likewise, near the end of Acts, Jesus' follower Paul is pronounced "innocent" of any crime by the Roman officer Claudius Lysias (Acts 23:29), by the Roman governor Festus (25:26), and by the Judean King Agrippa (Acts 26:32). The lesson is plain: those who follow Jesus are not political rebels, but are law abiding citizens working within the social order to make people's lives better.

Historical narrative is some of the most exciting material in the Bible, but to get its full impact, you have to ask the following questions:

- What does the writer repeatedly emphasize?
- Based on his own book, what was the intention of the writer?
- How does the writer's intention apply to me?

Studying Drama

The last type of literature we will examine in this chapter is often called "apocalyptic" in the commentaries, but I think the word "drama" best describes it in our own time. The term "apocalyptic" comes from Revelation 1:1, "The revelation of Jesus Christ, which God gave him to show his servants what must soon take place." The word "revelation" comes from the Greek word *apokalupsis*. Because the book of Revelation is so different from all the rest of the books of the Bible, Bible scholars recognized it as a separate type of literature. In creating a name for the literature, they took that Greek word, gave it an English format, and called it apocalyptic.

In every sense, however, the book of Revelation is really drama. Within the literature you will find "rivers of blood"; hailstones weighing a hundred pounds; a dragon so large he knocks down a third of the stars from the heavens; Death riding a horse; and a woman wearing the moon as a dress. These are exaggerated symbols for dramatic effect [see Ray Summers, *Worthy Is the Lamb: An Interpretation of Revelation* (Nashville, TN: Broadman, 1951), 25–26]. The literature is easily divided into acts and scenes (like a play) with music interspersed throughout.

For people used to reading fairly straightforward accounts in the historical, preaching, and letter sections of the Bible, the dramatic literature presented in the book of Revelation is something entirely different.

But it was not so different in the world of its origin. In fact, this kind of writing was quite common. I compare it to a modern *Star Wars* movie. The dramatic literature is found in a variety of places in the Bible, but the largest sample of it is found in Revelation. Therefore, we are going to center our attention on that book in order to discuss how to understand it.

Note: Stop your reading here and pick up your Bible. Read the book of Revelation through. Try to do it in one sitting. Picture what you read in your mind. Read for the "big picture." Imagine what the scenes would look like in a movie. Then, having read the book, come back to this chapter for the following guidelines.

First, recognize that the message of this book was not intended to be hidden or obscure. Remember, it is called the "revelation" of Jesus Christ. It can't be a "revelation" if it is not understood. In Revelation 1:3, Jesus said: "Blessed is the one who reads the words of this prophecy, and blessed are those who hear it and take to heart what is written in it . . . ." We can't take to heart something we don't understand. This book was written to be understood.

Second, like all the books of the Bible, it was written to be understood by its first readers. Interpretations that would not be understood by its original readers in the first century are not correct interpretations.

Third, like all the other books of the Bible, the book of Revelation has a point to make, and it is a point about behavior. Dramatic literature in the Bible was not intended as just an entertaining read. It was to impact a person's life. Dramatic literature provides a direction for living. But it does even more: dramatic literature is designed to motivate the reader to live the way it directs.

With these beginning principles, we turn to the book of Revelation itself.

It opens with the background to the book. This is section one (chapter 1). It tells us that the writer was John the apostle and that he is writing a message from Jesus. John says he received the message while imprisoned for his faith on the island of Patmos. John also says the message he received from Jesus is specifically addressed to seven congregations (or churches) scattered throughout ancient Asia—the area we know today as Turkey.

The book then moves into the message itself, section two (chapters 2–3), the directives for living. Each church is addressed in turn. Its good points are listed, along with its bad points. Each church is told what it needs to change and is encouraged to make the change by an appeal to blessing and judgment.

To emphasize the need for change and faithfulness, two motivational sections follow. Each of these sections begins and ends with a scene in heaven. That gives us our fourth guideline: note repetitions. See if they can be grouped to divide the book into smaller parts.

Section three includes chapters 4–11. This section, and the one to follow, repeat the same outline. They are designed to motivate Christian living. Each opens with a scene in heaven (chapters 4–5) followed by a scene of trouble on the earth for God's people (chapter 6). God takes note of the plight of his people and takes measures to protect them (chapter 7). Then God sets out to discipline the rest of the world in an attempt to get the world to turn to him (chapters 8–9). The Lord is unsuccessful in this attempt. In the end, God punishes the wicked with a judgment scene of lightning, thunder, and hail (chapters 10–11).

Section four (chapters 12–17) is much like section three. It begins with a scene in heaven (chapter 12) followed by a scene of trouble on the earth for God's people (chapter 13). God makes note of this and takes measures to protect his people (chapter 14) as he disciplines the rest of the world. This is an attempt to get the world to repent and turn to him (chapters 15 and 16).

Note how sections three and four correspond with one another. When you get to this point in each section, Jesus says virtually the same thing: "The rest of mankind that were not killed by these plagues still did not repent of the work of their hands; they did not stop worshiping demons, and idols of gold, silver, bronze, stone, and wood—idols that cannot see or hear or walk. Nor did they repent of their murders, their magic arts, their sexual immorality or their thefts" (compare Revelation 9:20–21 with 16:10–11). The section ends with a scene of God's victory pictured again with lightning, thunder, and earthquakes (16:17–21).

While we are on the subject of watching repetitions, sometimes things are repeated in different ways. Forty-two months and 1260 days are the same as three and a half years (see chapter 11).

Section five begins much the same way as four, with the voice of an angel inviting John to come and see something. In this case, it is a woman sitting on a red beast covered with unholy names. This brings us to our fifth guideline for reading dramatic literature. There are many symbols in this literature. But sometimes there are elements that are not symbols at all. Don't get too caught up in the images. The important images that are really symbols and have definite meaning are always explained. Look for the explanation. If it is not explained, don't worry about it. Likely, it is just costuming or scenery. In the case of the woman, she is identified as a city that sits on seven hills (Revelation 17:9). It is a city of power (18:10) and the first readers of Revelation would recognize her as the most powerful city in the ancient world—Rome. Through trade and other associations with her, other cities and people of the world had grown rich. But they had not grown spiritual. God's people are urged not to buy into the lifestyle of the movers and shakers of the world, but to "come out" so that God's people will not suffer as the rest of the world will suffer. Also identified in this section is the "dragon" (Satan 20:1–2), but throughout the book, other identifications are made (the seven lights before Jesus' feet are the seven churches being addressed—1:20). Like sections three and four, this one ends with a scene in heaven.

Dramatic literature has been a source of much division among believers, but the problem is mostly that readers have not read it as drama. The book was not written to offer clues to the timing of the end of the world. It was written to urge a particular lifestyle on the people of God. The lifestyle is explained.

The readers are motivated to embrace it. That's the message of the book about which we can all be certain.

6

Books of the Bible— Old Testament

Genesis

Genesis may well be the most important book in the Bible. It introduces us to God, tells us how humankind began, how sin began, and how the "people of God" began. It provides introductory insight into the justice, mercy, love, and grace of God and provides us an essential background for everything else in the Bible.

The main characters of Genesis are Adam and Eve, Noah, Abraham, his son Isaac, Isaac's son Jacob, and Jacob's son Joseph. The story begins in the fertile crescent of Mesopotamia and ends in the land of Egypt.

Nearly 400 years after the death of Jacob (also known as "Israel"), his family had grown from seventy to over a million. They were so numerous the Egyptians feared their nation and culture might be over-run and so they enslaved the people of Israel. God delivered them and brought them to the land he had promised Abraham. But by that time, Abraham had been dead over half a millennium and his descendants, before entering the promised land, needed to know something of their roots. At that point Moses wrote Genesis to tell them that story. Originally written in Hebrew, the Hebrew title of the book is "In the beginning."

Ten times in Genesis the author begins a new section with the words "This is the account" (or in some Bibles, "These are the generations"). The translation of that phrase into Greek gives us the word (in Greek) "Genesis" and that's where our title comes from. The book begins with God, and God is the prominent character throughout. I have divided it into five parts:

I)   God and the beginning 1:1–11:32
II) God and Abraham 12:1–21:7
III) God and Isaac 21:8–28:4
IV) God and Jacob 28:5–37:1
V)   God and Joseph 37:2–50:26

Genesis is important because, without it, you will not understand the significance of anything else in the Bible. In Genesis 12–13, God promised to make Abraham a great man and through his descendants bless all the nations of the world. Exodus through Deuteronomy tells how God made Israel a great nation. Joshua tells how God gave them a land. Judges through the end of the Old Testament recounts God's patience with his people and the blessedness and seriousness of their status. The Gospel accounts of the New Testament show how God ultimately extended his people to include those outside the Jewish nation. The book of Acts shows the fulfillment of that promise and the rest of the New Testament, down to the book of Revelation, deals with the lives of those people as they struggle (as Israel did) with their new status. The book of Revelation holds out hope to all who embrace God for a new heaven and earth where all struggle ceases and where the people of God dwell in his intimate presence forever.

Exodus

When Genesis ends, God seems to be everywhere. The story of Joseph, son of Jacob, is the longest personal narrative in Genesis and closes out the last thirteen chapters of the book. When Joseph was kidnapped and sold as a slave, the Bible says the Lord was with Joseph and caused him to prosper. When Joseph was falsely accused and imprisoned, the "Lord was with him and showed him kindness and granted him favor in the eyes of the prison warden" (Genesis 39:21). God caused Joseph to be released from prison and elevated him to second in command over all Egypt. God is there at every turn, and through all the hardships Joseph honored God with an exemplary life.

When Exodus begins, however, God seems nowhere to be found. Four hundred years pass between Genesis and Exodus, and as Exodus begins, all of God's people are enslaved. You can only imagine how the Israelites felt: God had let them down. While they had once been "the head and not the tail," they are now at the bottom.

But the story of Exodus affirms that God has not disappeared nor ceased watching over his people. In what will be the greatest story in the Old Testament, God delivers his people from Egyptian bondage so that they can worship him.

In the Hebrew Old Testament, Exodus is called "Names" from the first line of the book: "These are the names." Exodus 19:1 mentions "going out" of (or "exiting") Egypt, and when the

Old Testament was translated into Greek, this became the new name of the book. The book can be divided into four main parts.

I) God delivers the descendants of Jacob (known as the "Israelites" because Jacob's other name was "Israel"). Exodus 1:1–13:16.

II) Israel journeys under the protection of God to Sinai. Exodus 13:17–19:2

III) God tells Israel what he expects of them, both in how they live and how they approach him in worship. Exodus 19:3–34:28

IV) Israel's obedience to God illustrated in their building a place for worship. Exodus 34:29–40:38.

Sometimes our lives look and feel as if God is nowhere to be found. But he is there, planning our deliverance and bringing it to pass. That was surely the way it must have seemed for Jesus. Perhaps that's why his death is called, in the New Testament, an "Exodus" (or "departure" in Luke 9:31). And yet, God was there for him, just as he is for us. Between now and our own exodus, God calls us to a lifestyle that honors him in obedience and worships him in praise.

Leviticus

In the Hebrew Bible, the book of Leviticus is named "And He Called," which is the opening line of the book in Hebrew. When the Bible was translated into Greek, it became known as the "Book of the Levites." The Levites served in the priesthood of Old Testament Israel. When the Old Testament was translated into Latin, the book became "Leviticus," and the English name came from there.

God called all Israel to be a nation of priests (Exodus 19:6), but the people were not spiritually mature enough to function in that capacity. God therefore selected a group of Israelites, the tribe of Levi, to show the people what it meant to be priests for God. The regulations in Leviticus point to a priestly way of living that all Israel was expected to learn and respect.

A key term in Leviticus is the word "holy"; it is used more in Leviticus than any other book of the Bible. Generally meaning "separate," it is used specifically in the Bible to describe God. He is God, and there is no other god like him. When God called Israel to be holy, he called them to be unlike any other people, separate and distinct upon the earth. The book of Leviticus helped Israel to see what that meant. The book may be divided into three sections:

I)   Holy Things–Chapters 1–7 in which a system of sacrifice is detailed.
II) Holy People–Chapters 8–10 in which Aaron and his sons are consecrated as priests.
III) Holy Living–Chapters 11–27 in which lifestyle requirements are spelled out for God's holy people.

I urge you to keep two things in mind as you read this book. First, Leviticus reminds us of the seriousness of God's calling. We are not called to be like the rest of the world, nor are we allowed that option. Many have conjectured *why* God divided animals into clean and unclean, and why Israel had to be so scrupulous in observing that distinction. The last word has not been written on this subject, but I'm willing to believe God's distinction was arbitrary and without any rational basis. Observing the law was guaranteed to make the people Israel different from all other nations and the dietary laws reminded them at every meal and gathering that they couldn't "fit in" with the world.

Second, Leviticus prescribes very strict rules about approaching God in worship. God could be approached only in certain prescribed ways, otherwise disaster could be the result. Christians should always keep this in mind. The world cannot guide us in approaching God, for it knows little of his holiness.

New Testament writers use the language of Leviticus to refer to Jesus. He is our "sin offering" and "peace offering" and "High Priest." Israel's spiritual immaturity kept her from approaching God directly, forcing her to seek mediation with God through the priests. But in Christianity, the sacrifice of Jesus has made us all priests (1 Peter 2:5) and we all have bold access to God's throne of grace through Christ (Hebrews 4:16). Our lives must demonstrate, through holy living, our awareness of this great privilege we have.

Numbers

The Hebrew title for the fourth book of the Bible is "In the Wilderness," a much more appropriate title than Numbers, which doesn't tell us much about the book. Numbers begins in the second year after Israel's exodus from Egypt. It begins with a census of the people at Sinai and continues with Israel's move to enter the Promised Land. It gives us the details of her refusal to enter the land, and then provides us with a chronicle of her forty year wandering in punishment for disobedience. At the end of the forty years, there was another census (chapter 26) and a review of some of the laws Israel was to give attention to when she finally entered Canaan.

Every one of the first five books of the Bible serves to empha-size something about God. Genesis emphasizes his power and grace, Exodus his deliverance, Leviticus his holiness, and Deuteronomy his jealousy. Numbers is about God's presence.

Numbers can be divided into three sections:

I) Sinai (chapters 1–9) the census itself underscores God's presence and care. As he knows the very number of the hair on our heads, he knows exactly the number of people who belong to him. They don't move without him, and when they move he is there.

II) In the wilderness (chapters 10–21) contains the stories of at least seven rebellions against God. Though God had every reason to desert his people, he did not.

III) As Israel prepares to enter the land again (chapters 22–36), Moses tells Israel the story of an attempt to curse the people of God by a foreign nation. Through it all, unseen by Israel, God protected them.

Everyone numbered in the census of Israel was counted as a member of the community of God. God delivered Israel from Egypt to be one community. There are more references to that community in Numbers than in any other book of the Bible. The worst thing that could happen to anyone in Israel was to be placed outside the community, known in Numbers as "outside the camp."

Three thousand years after Moses, Numbers remains a rel-evant message to the people of God. The God who was a con-stant presence for Israel is a constant presence for us. He knows our number, and walks with us. He is present when we rebel, working out his will and protecting us in ways we cannot see. In a way, we are all traveling through the wilderness looking to enter the promised land. Until we do, we must allow God to be our leader and guide, and we must, as the church, stick together as the people of God.

How did the title Numbers come about? When the Old Testament was translated into Greek, then Latin, those census reports stood out in the translators' minds. The Greeks called it *arithmoi*, and in Latin it became *Numeri*. From there, it was but a short hop to Numbers in English.

Deuteronomy

Chuck Swindoll (citing D. L. Moody) says that Moses spent his first forty years thinking he was a somebody, the next forty learning he was a nobody, and his final forty learning what God can do with a nobody [Charles Swindoll, *Moses: A Man of Selfless Dedication* (Word Publishing, 1999), 20]. It was near the end of these last forty years that Moses spoke the words we find in the book of Deuteronomy. The late Peter Craigie, Bible scholar and former vice president of the University of Calgary, wrote: "Deuteronomy is a book about a community being prepared for a new life. Hardship and wilderness lie behind; the promised land lies ahead. But in the present moment, there is a call for a new commitment to God and a fresh understanding of the nature of the community of God's people. . . . [I]n the midst of world events, a relatively small community was being urged by Moses, the 'man of God,' to commit itself wholeheartedly to the Lord, before engaging in the struggle for the promised land" [Peter C. Craigie, *The Book of Deuteronomy* (Eerdmans, 1976), 7].

Deuteronomy contains five speeches of Moses and begins with the line "These are the words . . . ." That is, in fact, the Hebrew title of the book. The English title comes from a later Greek translation of Deuteronomy 17:18 where the king is commanded to make a copy of the law of God. The translation made the text say the king was to make a "second" law, a *deuteronomion* to keep with him and be his guide. This word was carried over into the Latin translation and continued into English.

I)   Deuteronomy begins (chapters 1–4) with a call to justice and a review of how Israel came to be east of the Jordan river in the territory of Moab. Moses reviews Israel's failures and successes and points out that they owe every success to God. Moses wants Israel to know that God is serious about them being his people, and Moses reminds them all (five times) that, despite the fact he has been with Israel since they left Egypt, he will not get to enter the promised land. The reason is due to his own failure—and Israel's.

II) Chapters 5–11 set forth the law of God in an abbreviated form (the Ten Commandments) and call Israel to obedience. The Ten Commandments serve as a foundation for all the laws of God. The Ten Commandments were spoken directly to Israel by God, and written by God personally on stone.

III) Chapters 12–26 provide an elaboration of the Ten Commandments, showing how the commands apply in a broad sense.

IV) Chapters 27–28 list curses for those who do not follow the law of God, and blessings for those who do.

V) Chapters 29–34 is a final call to faithfulness and concludes with the death of Moses.

Obedience is paramount in Deuteronomy. Israel should obey, not in order to receive the promises, but in order to keep from losing them. This is a significant point. The false doctrine of salvation by works does not *just* teach that works are involved in salvation. It teaches that *by* one's works one can *secure* salvation. The people of Israel, however, had already been saved by God's grace. If they wanted to *stay* saved, and wanted their lives to go well, they would have to be obedient. The same is true of us. Again, as Peter Craigie puts it: Deuteronomy "provides a paradigm for the kingdom of God in the modern world; it is time for renewing commitment within the New Covenant and turning to the future with a view to possessing the promise of God" (Craigie, *The Book of Deuteronomy*, 7).

Joshua

Moses died on Mt. Nebo and God buried him in Moab, "in the valley opposite Beth Peor." Up to that time Moses was the only leader the nation of Israel had ever known. God allowed Israel to grieve for thirty days, and then said to them all: "Moses is dead. It's time to go."

Joshua, Moses' assistant, took his place and the book that bears his name covers his leadership in the invasion, conquest, and occupation of the land of Canaan.

The name "Joshua" means "The Lord is Salvation." Richard Hess writes: "The book of Joshua is foremost the story of God, who works powerfully on behalf of Israel and Joshua, fulfilling His covenant promises. It is God who leads Israel across the Jordan, defeats Israel's enemies and presides over the apportionment of the land. And so, in the final chapter, it is God who receives Israel's worshipful re-commitment at Shechem" [Richard S. Hess, *Joshua* (Downers Grove, IL: IVP, 1996)].

The book is called "Joshua," and it says Joshua recorded the events in the "Book of the Law of God." But I have wondered whether Joshua actually wrote the book of Joshua (no text actually says he did—he's just the main character). There are things in it Joshua likely *wouldn't* have written, like this passage in Joshua 24: "After these things, Joshua son of Nun, the servant of the LORD, died at the age of a hundred and ten. And they buried him in the land of his inheritance, at Timnath Serah in the hill country of Ephraim, north of Mount Gaash. Israel served the LORD throughout the lifetime of Joshua and of the elders who outlived him and who had experienced everything the LORD had done for Israel."

Notice the last phrase. It points us to a time *after* Joshua's death and *after* the death of the leading men of Joshua's day. Additionally, the writer points to proofs confirming his story that remain to his own time ("to this day"—the phrase occurs eleven times in the book). This is an important point. The account found in Joshua is a true account, as evidenced by the author's references to the "proofs" of the stories that the reader could "check out" for himself. Likely, the stories themselves were originally written by Joshua. But the final form of the book was prepared by someone *other* than Joshua.

More important, however, than the author is this question: why was the book written?

Everything from Genesis to Deuteronomy points to an unrealized promise of God: that he would give the descendants of Abraham a land of their own. This promise becomes a reality in the story of Joshua. Four hundred years before, Joseph had reminded his family of the promise, and made them commit to burying him in Shechem when the promise came true. Joshua ends with the story of Joseph's burial at Shechem and with reminders that "not one of the Lord's good promises to the house of Israel failed, every one was fulfilled" (21:45 and see 22:4; 23:14–15). The message for Israel in Joshua was that God is with his people and he will keep his word to them. They, in turn, must be obedient.

It is a message every generation of God's people would do well to hear and follow. Joshua can be outlined as follows:

I) Conquest of the land (Joshua 1–12)
II) Allotment of the land (Joshua 13–22)
III) A call to faithfulness (Joshua 23–24)

Judges and Ruth

After the occupation of the Promised Land, Israel existed as a loose confederation of tribes. Her scandalous disunity is one of the themes of the book of Judges. Reading that story, no one can doubt that these were the darkest days of Israel's history.

Throughout Judges, a specific cycle of events repeats itself twelve times:

1) God causes Israel to prosper.

2) Israel, in her prosperity, turns from God to find acceptance from the pagan people around her. God had warned her about this: "Be careful that you do not forget the LORD your God . . . otherwise, when you eat and are satisfied, when you build fine houses and settle down, and when your herds and flocks grow large and your silver and gold increase and all you have is multiplied, then your heart will become proud and you will forget the LORD your God . . . . You may say to yourself, 'My power and the strength of my hands have produced this wealth for me.' But remember the LORD your God, for it is he who gives you the ability to produce wealth, and so confirms his covenant, which he swore to your forefathers, as it is today" (Deuteronomy 8:11–19). Not much has changed along this line since the days of the Judges.

3) God, punishing Israel for her unfaithfulness, causes her to be oppressed so that she will return to God.

4) Israel repents and turns back to God.

5) God raises up a judge, a leader, who delivers Israel and restores peace.

Judges may be outlined as follows:

I) Introduction to the times—chapters 1–2
II) The oppressions of God's people—chapters 3–16
III) Social collapse and the call for leadership—chapters 17–21

Note the last section in this outline. The writer's ultimate point is the need for leadership among the people of God, and it must be righteous leadership. Four times in the last section the writer points out that there was no king in Israel, and twice he adds that everyone did what was right in his own eyes. God had always wanted to be Israel's king, but she would not submit to him and her success became checkered at best.

It wasn't *just* a lack of leadership. It was also Israel's tendency to assimilate with the people of the surrounding countries. She wanted to be accepted by the people around her, and she often sacrificed God's holiness for the world's approval. The message of Judges for us is that this hunger for the world's approval will bring God's discipline. Our leaders in the church must be people dedicated to God, and we must stick together and follow them.

As the book of Judges draws to a close, the scenes of Israel's collapse are gruesome and shocking. An Israelite creates his own religion. Priests are bought by individuals and tribes as good luck charms. Innocent and helpless people are murdered. A woman is gang raped and killed, and then dismembered by her husband and her body parts sent throughout Israel as a protest against those crimes. This is the destiny of every society that refuses to yield to God and chooses instead to allow every person to do what is right in his own eyes.

Everything looks hopeless.

But the small book of Ruth picks up the story and shows how God can turn things around.

An Israelite man and his family move from Israel to Moab to escape a famine. His two sons married Moabite women (against the law of God—1 Kings 11:2). In time the man and his sons died. His widow, Naomi, and one of her daughters-in-law, Ruth, return to the land of Israel (all in chapter 1). There Ruth meets an Israelite, Boaz, the descendant of a well-known prostitute. Chapters 2–4 detail their courtship and marriage, but most important of all, the text concludes with the note that these are the ancestors of Israel's greatest King, David.

The point is, when things look the bleakest for God's people, God is still working among them to bring about his purpose and blessing.

1 & 2 Samuel

The books of Samuel were originally one book. They were separated into two documents when translated into Greek in the third century BC. That separation continued into our English Bibles. The Hebrew Bible kept them united until the appearance of the first printed edition about 500 years ago. In the Greek translation, Samuel was known as First and Second Kingdoms, a designation that continued until the Latin Bible of the fourth century AD (and can be seen in the King James Bible's title: "The First Book of Samuel, otherwise called The First Book of Kings). The Hebrew Bible kept the designation Samuel.

The most crucial question to ask when studying the books of Samuel, Kings, and Chronicles is: "Why were these books written?" It is, however, the question most often left unasked. The books are normally read and taught as books of history chronicling the period of the Israelite monarchy. That approach leaves us to draw whatever conclusions we see fit from the stories presented, causing us to miss the central theme.

First and Second Samuel are named for the central character at the beginning of the first book. In the list of judges of Israel, Samuel is the last. He is also the means by which God anoints the first two kings, Saul and David. The books of Samuel may be outlined as follows:

I)   Samuel (1 Samuel 1–7)
II) Saul (1 Samuel 8–15)
III) Saul and David (1 Samuel 16–31)
IV) David (2 Samuel)

David was considered the greatest king of Israel. In fact, the writer of the book of Chronicles evaluates the kings of Judah by comparing them with David. Yet Samuel does not present a flattering picture of David or his predecessor Saul.

Samuel opens with the failure of Eli (Israel's 14th Judge) to lead his own house and Israel. Samuel, Eli's successor, begins with great promise, but his story ends in a similar way, with Samuel's inability to lead both God's people and his own family. The story of Saul begins with great promise, but ends in failure. In fact, most of the account of Saul's reign deals with his rebellion against God. The story of David likewise begins with great promise, but his reign is checkered with failure. In fact, the largest single section of Samuel tells of David's adultery (unmentioned by the writer of Chronicles) and the resultant rebellion in his family. Like Eli and Samuel before him, David failed as a leader in his own house. Like Saul, David failed often as a leader of Israel. But unlike Saul, Samuel, or Eli, David is presented as a "man after God's own heart." What was the difference?

The great comparison is between David and Saul, and the difference has to do with their relationship with God. Three stories occupy the bulk of Saul's reign: his war with the Philistines, the near murder of his son, and his war with the Amalekites (1 Samuel 13–15). In each story, Saul is either unconcerned with the will of God or blatantly disobedient. The longest section of David's reign likewise tells a story of failure and disobedience, but the difference between Saul and David is that David cares most of all what God thinks about him, and ultimately always seeks forgiveness and God's approval. In the long story of David's rebelling family, we find this heart-warming assessment of God: "Like water spilled on the ground, which cannot be recovered, so we must die. But God does not take away life; instead, he devises a way so that a banished person may not remain estranged from him" (2 Samuel 14:14).

Judges described the darkest part of Israel's history. It calls for a king to lead the people. But Samuel points out that a king is not the answer, for the darkness of the days does not disappear with the rule of a king. What is needed is a changed heart. This will be the key to God's blessing and approval.

1 and 2 Kings

Like Samuel, the Old Testament books of Kings were originally one book, separated when the Old Testament was translated into Greek in the second century BC. Like Samuel, we do not know the author of Kings. Also like Samuel, the most important question in studying the book is: "Why was this book written?"

Though we do not have an exact date for the writing of Kings, it would have been no earlier than 560 BC and certainly after the death of Jehoiachin, king of Judah, a few years later.

Samuel ends with David, king of Israel. Kings picks up with David's last years, his death (cir. 928 BC), and the ascension of his son Solomon to the throne. Chapters 2–11 deal with Solomon's reign, most of it (chapters 5–8) focused on the building of the temple of God in Jerusalem . At Solomon's death, his son Rehoboam became king. Solomon's reign had not served to unite God's people, and at the ascension of Rehoboam God's people divided into two nations: a "North" (Israel) and a "South" (Judah). From 1 Kings 12 to 2 Kings 17, the story is of two nations. In 2 Kings 17, the northern kingdom is destroyed by the Assyrians. In 2 Kings 25, the end of the book, the southern Kingdom is destroyed and its people carted off into exile in Babylon.

The message of 1 and 2 Kings is plain: the end of these nations was the result of their rebellion against God. An outline of the books is as follows:

1) Death of David and reign of Solomon—1 Kings 1–11
2) Creation of the Northern Kingdom and its first seven kings (beginning with Jeroboam).—1 Kings 12–16.
3) Ministry of Elijah—1 Kings 16–2 Kings 1
4) Ministry of Elisha—2 Kings 2–13
5) Final seven kings of the Northern Kingdom—2 Kings 14–17 (beginning with Jeroboam II)
6) Final kings of the Southern Kingdom—2 Kings 18–25

The people who would have first read Kings were Jews in Babylonian exile. At that time, the nation of Israel had not existed as a people for nearly 200 years. We have to wonder why so much of the book (27 out of 47 chapters) is devoted to this long-gone nation? And why is there so much emphasis on the "prophets"? (one-third of the book is devoted to the ministries of Elijah and Elisha.) Why are the reigns of the kings so disproportionate? Omri, who founded Samaria, ruled twelve years, and was the greatest political mind of the Northern Kingdom, gets only six verses. Jeroboam II, who ushered in the golden age of the Northern Kingdom, gets seven verses. Manasseh, who ruled Judah fifty-five years, gets eighteen verses. But Hezekiah, King of Judah, known for his faithfulness to God, gets three chapters.

The first recipients of this book needed to know why they lived in Babylon. Kings tells them it is because of their sins, and the consequence of the sins of their forefathers. They need hope for the future. Solomon's prayer at the temple dedication speaks of a time of exile for sin, and the possibility of return if the people will repent and turn to God (1 Kings 8:46ff). The first readers needed direction. The word of the prophets called people to holiness. No one paid attention, and destruction was the result. The Northern Kingdom was an example. The Southern Kingdom is being given a second chance. But if they do not heed the words of the prophets, their doom is assured.

As we read Kings, we need to hear its message afresh. Neither politics nor the most astute political leaders can assure peace and prosperity or thwart the judgment of God when his people stop paying attention to his direction. And not even the existence of a magnificent temple devoted to the Lord will protect them if the lives of those who worship there are characterized by rebellion and worldliness. Four chapters are devoted to the building of the temple. God burns it to the ground in one verse at the end of the book. Within one generation of the writing of Kings, the exiles will return to Judah to rebuild. Their future will be determined by their faithfulness.

1 and 2 Chronicles

The books of Kings are often called a "synchronistic history" because they present both the story of the Northern Kingdom of Israel and the Southern Kingdom of Judah at the same time. It "synchronizes" their stories, switching back and forth between them as if to say, 'While all this was going on in the north, this was going on in the south.' Though 1 and 2 Chronicles present an account of the same time frame, the main story has to do only with the south.

Chronicles appears as the last book in the Hebrew Bible. In Hebrew, it is called "Words of Days." When it was translated into Greek, the translators called it "Things Left Out" (meaning things left out of the other historical books). In the fourth century AD, the Christian scholar Jerome noted that Chronicles begins not with David, but with Adam, and he called the book in Latin "The Chronicle of the Whole of Sacred History." That name stuck and today it is called Chronicles. It is the third longest book in the Old Testament. Again, the most important question in a study of this book is: "Why was it written?"

Chronicles was written sometime after 532 BC because the last thing mentioned in it is that date. That was the date of the return of the Jewish people from Babylonian exile to rebuild Jerusalem and their temple. Whatever message is in this book, it is for those returning exiles.

The writer of Chronicles covers the history of the world from Adam to Saul, the first king of Israel, in the opening nine chapters. He does so simply through genealogy. Along the way, interspersed through the genealogies, he makes a few side comments. Jabez prayed and God heard his prayer (4:9–10). Reuben, Jacob's firstborn, lost his birthright because of immorality (5:1–2). Three tribes went to war with four ancient nations and won because they prayed to God (5:18–22). A half tribe was destroyed by the Assyrians because of their wickedness (5:24–26).

You get the picture: from the beginning of time, success has depended on a faithfull relationship with God. As the book progresses, David is held up as the example for everyone else (David's failures—his sin with Bathsheba, for example—are not mentioned). The kings of Judah are compared with David. Those who compare well are good. Those who do not, are not.

Chronicles focuses on God's faithfulness when his people turn to him. First, over and over are references to the trustworthiness of God's promises. Second, from 2 Chronicles 10–36, there are some forty-six references to prayer. In Kings, Manasseh is portrayed as a horrible king. But in Chronicles, Manasseh is one whose prayers God heard when he called to the Lord. God says: "If my people, who are called by my name, will humble themselves and pray and seek my face and turn from their wicked ways, then will I hear from heaven and will forgive their sin and will heal their land" (2 Chronicles 7:14). That promise will be important to exiles returning to rebuild their lives and their nation.

Chronicles still speaks to the people of God. No matter their relationship, God will not tolerate wickedness forever. At some point, a lack of repentance will bring judgment. But despite the judgment, God loves forever. He seeks a renewed relationship with his people, and they are never so far from him that when they call he will not hear or come to their aid—not even when they are exiled a thousand miles away in Babylon. The returning exiles needed that assurance, and God, through the history of the Jewish people in Chronicles, provided it to them. The message remains just as valid for us, who are now called by the name of his son, Jesus the Christ.

Ezra and Nehemiah

For 400 years the Jewish people lived under the rule of judges. After that—about 1000 BC—they were ruled by kings: first by Saul, then David, then Solomon. At Solomon's death, the kingdom was divided into two parts: a north called Israel, and a south called Judah. From Solomon's death until 722 BC, nineteen kings ruled in the north and thirteen ruled in the south. Both empires had great difficulty remaining true to God, and Israel found it most difficult—so much so that in 722 BC, God had the northern empire destroyed because of their sinfulness. An account of all these kings may be found in the book of Kings.

The southern kingdom of Judah continued a history of spotty faithfulness to God. Seven more kings ruled until 586 BC when the nation was overcome by the Babylonians and displaced to Mesopotamia (this period is covered both by the books of Kings and the books of Chronicles). Centuries before, God warned Judah this would happen (Isaiah 39:5–7). He also promised their captivity would last seventy years, after which they would be released (Jeremiah 29:10–14).

By 539 BC, the Persian King Cyrus had conquered the Babylonians and, as God had promised, permitted the Jews to return to their homeland. Ezra begins to chronicle that return. Nearly 50,000 people made the first migration back to Judea; they immediately set about rebuilding the temple the Babylonians had destroyed half a century earlier. It was tough going. Facing outside opposition and overcome by materialism and a flagging interest in God, it took nearly twenty years to complete the rebuilding. Possession of a temple, however, will not make a spiritual people. What they needed was a spiritual leader, and God provided that in the person of Ezra, who appears for the first time in chapter 7 of the book that bears his name.

Ezra was a direct descendant of Aaron, the first high priest of Israel. He was a good man, "well versed in the law of Moses." So spiritual was he that when he learned of the great sins that beset the Jewish people in Judea, he tore his robes and pulled hair from his head and beard. The last four chapters deal with the spiritual reforms Ezra put in place among the people. In an age such as our own, where we often preach "come as you are" in our calls to discipleship, these final chapters pointedly and painfully show what changes God may require to make our lifestyles acceptable to him *after* we come as we are.

Traditionally, in the Hebrew Bible, Ezra and Nehemiah were considered one book. After the return of the Jews in Ezra, the rebuilding of the temple, and the enacting of spiritual reforms, what the Jewish people needed was a political leader. God provided him in the person of Nehemiah. His book recounts Nehemiah's reforms and his rebuilding of the city of Jerusalem. Nehemiah was a spiritual man, but he was also a political figure. He would ensure, by force if necessary, that God's people were obedient to God's law.

With the return of the exiles, the rebuilding of the temple, the instituting of religious revival, and the establishing of a stable and righteous government, you would think the Jews would be well on their way to holiness. This was not the case.

Nehemiah ruled in Jerusalem for twelve years before returning to the service of the king of Persia. Some time after that, he returned to Jerusalem to discover God's people had resumed their faithless ways.

It is at this point, at the end of Nehemiah, that the history covered by the Old Testament comes to an end. There are more books to be sure, but the span of the story is over.

Ezra and Nehemiah tell the story of the faithfulness of God to the unfaithful people he loves. Ezra attempted spiritual reform through teaching and example. Nehemiah attempted spiritual reform through spiritual leadership and force. Both ways failed in the long run. If the people of God are going to live like the people of God, the reform must come, not just from the outside, but from within our hearts.

Esther

When Israel left Egypt during the Exodus, God eventually brought them to the Plains of Moab, just east of the Jordan river. There Moses, in five presentations preserved for us in Deuteronomy, urged the people of God to be faithful to the Lord. In fact, Deuteronomy 28 contains some of the harshest language about unfaithfulness to be found in the Bible. If Israel did not obey, God said they would be cursed everywhere they went. They would feel crushed by both earth and sky, and God would afflict them with madness, blindness, and confusion of mind (vss. 28, 34). A foreign nation would invade them and carry them to a land far away. God would ruin them, destroy them, and scatter them.

The promised blessings and cursings were to be inscribed on monuments located in the center of the land, but Israel still failed to pay attention to them. In 605 BC, the Babylonians invaded Israel and carried off many in the royal family as hostages (like Daniel). In 597 BC, the Babylonians returned to carry off more of them (Ezekiel was among this group). In 586 BC, the Babylonians returned for the final time to destroy Jerusalem and carry off the remaining citizenry.

But even in God's harshest language, he never promised his people would be totally wiped out. The expectation was that God would allow some to survive. Ezra and Nehemiah recount the story of the rebuilding of the nation of Israel by survivors of the Babylonian exile. The period extends from 539 BC to 433 BC and between the stories of Ezra and Nehemiah, the story of Esther takes place. Ezra and Nehemiah tell us about those who returned to Judea. Esther tells us about those who remained behind.

One of the enduring themes of the Old Testament is the high position Israel enjoyed *just because she was the people of God*. Whoever criticized or hurt the people of God—even if they deserved it—suffered for it. Israel was the "apple" of God's eye (Zechariah 2:8) and no one touched her without suffering retribution. You see this protection and exalted status in the story of Esther.

There are four main characters in the story. *Xerxes* is the great Persian king who, while a military master, was pretty inept as a human being. In a drunken stupor he made a poor decision that caused trouble between him and his wife. Then he listened to poor advisors and divorced his wife and began to look for another.

The second character is *Haman*, a descendant of Agag, king of the Amalekites, constant enemies of Israel. Haman had become an important man in the Persian empire, and he determined to use his position to exterminate the Jews.

The third character is *Mordecai*, a good Jew who takes his cousin Esther into his home and raises her when her parents die. Mordecai has the good fortune to be at the right place at the right time to foil an assassination attempt against Xerxes.

The fourth character is *Esther*, a young woman whose character and personality won the hearts of everyone who met her. When the king went looking for a new wife, Esther was one of the ones brought to him. Because of the strong anti-Jewish sentiment in Persia, Mordecai had insisted Esther keep her Jewish identity a secret.

The story of Esther is the story of how a most unlikely person (a Jewish orphan) becomes the queen of Persia and foils a plot, hatched by the second most powerful man in the world, to exterminate the people of God. It provides for us the background to the Jewish festival of Purim that commemorates the event.

One of the amazing things about this book is the absence of God. Nowhere is God even mentioned. But no one familiar with the literature of the Old Testament can fail to see the similarity between this story and the stories of Joseph and Moses—all showing that God often works in ordinary ways through ordinary folk to protect the people he loves.

Job

If not the oldest book in the Bible, Job certainly reaches back to the earliest of times—to the days of Abraham or before. The book tells the story of man named Job whose fortunes went from great to abysmal virtually overnight simply because of a conflict between Satan and God. The story of Job is set at a time when a family's patriarch offered sacrifices on behalf of his children. Job is not listed in any of the genealogies of Abraham's descendants and therefore he is not a part of Israel. He is from the land of Uz, a place whose geographical location is unknown.

Despite not being a Jew and of unknown origin, the story of Job's faith is a treasure of Jewish literature. He is considered in the Old Testament to be one of three most righteous people (Daniel and Noah being the other two—cf. Ezekiel 14:14, 20).

Chapters 1–3 set the stage for the story and introduce us to all the players but one. Job is a righteous man, well-blessed by God with everything a man can desire: wealth, respect in the community, family, and a close relationship with God. He is "the greatest man among all the people of the East." God brags to Satan: "Have you considered my servant Job? There is no one on earth like him; he is blameless and upright, a man who fears God and shuns evil."

It sounds more like a taunt to Satan. Satan replies: "Sure he's good. Why shouldn't he be? You've bought his goodness with all your blessings. Take them away, and he will curse you to your face."

And so the conflict begins. God allows Satan to strip Job of everything, including his dignity. Job doesn't know that he has become a pawn in a holy war. He's just confused that such awful things have happened. Despite them, however, and despite encouragement from his wife to turn from God, Job remains true. He said: "Naked I came from my mother's womb, and naked I will depart. The LORD gave and the LORD has taken away; may the name of the LORD be praised."

Three of Job's friends, Eliphaz, Bildad, and Zophar, come to provide support; the condition they find him in leaves them speechless, at least at first. For Job's part, he wishes he had never been born.

Chapters 4–31 contain three rounds of speeches where each of Job's friends speak, trying to put things into perspective. Job replies to each of them. Eliphaz urges him to put his trust in God, but Job replies that God is the reason he is in this mess. Bildad and Zophar both reply that it's not God's fault, but Job's.

All three of the friends subscribe to the world view that if something bad happens to you, it must be your fault. Job believes the same thing, but he does not see how *this* is *his* fault. He concludes that God must have attacked him.

In chapters 32–37 a new much younger character, Elihu, appears. He is upset the others have not convinced Job all this is not God's fault. He maintains that sometimes bad things happen so that God can speak to our lives. Job does not reply to Elihu.

Then God himself takes the stage. In two speeches (chapters 38–41), God says, first, that there are some things humans cannot know. Second, because their knowledge is limited, they should be slow to blame God for everything that happens.

The book ends (chapter 42) with God restoring everything Job lost.

Job's friends never prayed for Job. They never encouraged him. They never comforted him. Job felt badly toward God, but he never turned from him. Even if, for some unknown reason, God was attacking him, Job's only hope was still in God. To turn from the only one who could deliver him would have been foolish.

Will a person serve God for nothing? The book of Job says the righteous person will do exactly that. When you are going through a difficult time, there is something more important than *why* all that is happening to you. It is more important to entrust your life to the one who knows everything and who has assured us, one way or another, he will deliver us. That's what Jesus did. "During the days of Jesus' life on earth, he offered up prayers and petitions with loud cries and tears to the one who could save him from death, and he was heard because of his reverent submission" (Hebrews 5:7).

Psalms (1)

The book of Psalms is sometimes called the "Hebrew Song Book." With its 150 chapters, it is the longest single body of literature in the Old Testament. Unlike other books of the Bible, each chapter of the Psalms is an independent literary unit and the whole is a compilation of poetry that spans a thousand years. Though most of the poems were written by Israel's greatest king, David, other poems were written by Moses, Solomon, Asaph (who was in charge of the music of the tabernacle in David's day), the sons of Korah (guardians of the temple gates), and some rather obscure fellows like Jeduthun and Heman.

The book of Psalms is divided into five "books," each one ending with praise to God:

1) Book 1—Psalm 1–41, ending with "Praise be to the Lord, the God of Israel, from everlasting to everlasting. Amen and Amen."

2) Book 2—Psalms 42–72, ending with "Praise be to the Lord God, the God of Israel, who alone does marvelous deeds. Praise be to his glorious name forever; may the whole earth be filled with his glory. Amen and Amen."

3) Book 3—Psalms 73–89, ending with "Praise be to the Lord forever! Amen and Amen."

4) Book 4—Psalms 90–106, ending with "Praise be to the Lord, the God of Israel, from everlasting to everlasting. Let all the people say, 'Amen!' Praise the Lord."

5) Book 5—Psalms 107–150, ending with an entire psalm of praise.

116 of the Psalms have headings. We do not know if these headings were on the original manuscripts, but the headings appear in all the manuscripts we have. The headings tell who wrote the psalm, sometimes its occasion, and sometimes the tune it was to be sung to. Unfortunately, the tunes are now lost to us.

Psalms contains some repetition. Psalm 14 is repeated in Psalm 53. Psalm 57 is repeated in Psalm 108. Psalm 40 is repeated in Psalm 70. Why the repetition? I do not know. We know that these were not the only pieces of poetry written by Old Testament people. Solomon himself wrote a thousand and five songs. David likely wrote many more than those catalogued in the book of Psalms. It may well be that the five books of psalms we have represent five collections of psalms. Just as today, different editions of hymn books contain different collections, and some repetitions, so that may be equally true with Psalms.

In the sixteenth century, John Calvin wrote: "I have been wont to call this book, not inappropriately, an anatomy of all parts of the soul; for there is not an emotion of which anyone can be conscious that is not here represented in a mirror."

John Hus, a Christian leader in fourteenth-century Europe, spoke out strongly against what amounted to the sale of forgiveness of sins. The penalty for speaking out against the church at the time was beheading, but since Hus was a respected leader, he was simply excommunicated. Later, he was tried for heresy, forbidden to defend himself, and sentenced to be burned alive, tied to a stake. As he walked to his execution, he recited these words from the Psalm 31: "In you, O Lord, I have taken refuge; let me never be put to shame; deliver me in your righteousness. . . Into your hands I commit my spirit; redeem me, O Lord, the

God of truth." Jesus, on the cross, cited the same psalm. The first Christian martyr, Stephen, also cited it as he was being stoned.

Psalms (2)

The longest book of the Bible is the book of Psalms. It is the most cited Old Testament book by New Testament writers (but Isaiah runs a close second). Walter Brueggemann has written: "In season and out of season, generation after generation, faithful women and men turn to the Psalms as a most helpful resource for conversation with God about things that matter most" [Walter Brueggemann, *The Message of the Psalms* (Minneapolis, MN: Augsburg, 1984), 15]. He divides the Psalms into three categories:

1) Psalms of *orientation*. I call these "good time psalms," expressions of the heart when times are going well.
2) Psalms of *disorientation*. These are the "bad times psalms," expressions of the heart when things are not going well. There is hurt, separation, suffering, and death. Life is ragged. The largest number of psalms are of this type. (Wonder why that is?)
3) Psalms of *reorientation*, which I call "turn-around psalms." Things have been going poorly, but life has changed and is now headed in a new and better direction.

Of all the Psalms, perhaps none has provided Christians with as much difficulty as those called the Imprecatory Psalms. These are prayers that ask God to do horrible things to other people. The most notable are Psalms 55, 59, 69, 79, 109, and 137. How could a person of God ask God to "let death take my enemies by surprise" or make their eyes "darkened so they cannot see and their backs bent forever"? Is it really appropriate for us to pray: "Pour out your wrath on the nations that do not acknowledge you, on the kingdoms that do not call on your name"?

We are much more comfortable with Jesus' and Stephen's prayer for their enemies: "Do not hold this sin against them."

While we would like to pray Jesus' prayer, and while it is surely more in keeping with his command to love our enemies and pray for those who persecute us (Matthew 5:43ff), it is nevertheless true that there are times justice seems so trampled on that the imprecatory psalms more accurately reflect the feelings of our heart. The book of Psalms is God's word to us that whatever we feel about ourselves, about others, and even about God, none of those feelings are new or unique to us. Great people of God have felt them too. And when they had those feelings, good or bad, joyful or sad, convicted or confused, they didn't take matters into their own hands. They took their feelings to God. As much as anything else, the book of Psalms provides us with the vocabulary to unburden our heart and approach God in any season of life.

In the fourth century AD, Ambrose, a preacher and elder of the church in Milan, Italy, wrote: "Although all scripture breathes the grace of God, yet sweeter than all the others is the book of Psalms. History instructs, the Law teaches, Prophecy announces, rebukes, chastens, and morality persuades. But in the book of Psalms, we have the fruit of these—and a kind of medicine for the salvation of men." More near our own time, Walter Brueggemann (whom we mentioned earlier) has written: "The Psalms draw our entire life under the rule of God, where everything may be submitted to the God of the gospel" (*The Message of the Psalms*, 15).

Proverbs

"Well done is better than well said."

"God helps those who help themselves."

"Early to bed, early to rise, makes a man healthy, wealthy, and wise."

These are but a few of our "American proverbs," all of which came, at least through, if not from, Benjamin Franklin.

Every culture has its proverbs. From Babylon during the days of Abraham we have the following: "Build like a Lord, live like a slave. Build like a slave, live like a Lord." From Egypt we have this one: "A petitioner likes attention to his words better than the fulfilling of that for which he came . . . a good hearing is a soothing of the heart."

The culture of Israel in the Old Testament was no different. Solomon himself was said to have spoken three thousand proverbs, and over 300 of them are specifically to be found in the book of Proverbs, part of what is called the "wisdom literature" of the Old Testament. The book of Proverbs has more parallels with ancient literature than any other book in the Bible.

Proverbs has little organizational structure, but may be outlined as follows:

I)   Title and aim of the book. 1:1–7
II) The importance of wisdom. 1:8–9:18
III) Proverbs of Solomon (374 two liners)—10:1–22:16
IV) Sayings of other wise men—22:17–24:22

V)   Hezekiah's collection of Solomon's proverbs—25–29
VI) Wisdom from the wise man Agur—30
VII) Wisdom from King Lemuel—31:1–9
VIII) The Woman of Noble character—31:10–31

Wisdom has to do with "how" we live our lives in order to be successful. Proverbs are wise rules of conduct. They are not guarantees. Our proverb, "Early to bed, early to rise, makes a man healthy, wealthy, and wise," is a good rule to follow, but not a guarantee. Some labor from dawn to dusk, destroy their health, and never become wealthy. But on the other hand, "Go to bed late, get up late," is a prescription for disaster.

Since they are not guarantees, they should not be read or treated as laws. Thus the parent who "trains up his child in the way he should go" can *expect* that his child will live accordingly. But that is not a guarantee. If a child turns from the wise path later in life, it should not serve as an indictment against the parents. On the other hand, of course, the parent who offers no guidance for his child can fairly well expect him to turn out poorly.

Proverbs offers direction for daily manners, work, sex, family life, friendship, and relationship with God. These particular proverbs are important because they come to us by the approval of God and as such, provide us not just with earthly wisdom, but heavenly.

Ecclesiastes

"That's got to be the most depressing book of the Bible. Just read it: 'Meaningless, meaningless . . . utterly meaningless! Everything is meaningless' And that's just the first two verses!"

My friend was talking about Ecclesiastes, of course.

But Ecclesiastes was not intended to be depressing. It *was* intended to be a sobering look at life. Listening to the radio one morning, I heard a news segment on how much banks charge in fees. A young girl complained that she over-drew her account by $5 and the bank charged her $25. She said: "It's as if they are sucking the money from our accounts." I thought: "You knew that going in young lady. You are the one over-drawing your account. You only have yourself to blame."

Not very compassionate of me, right? (Actually, I *do* feel for her. The charges are excessive. But the charges are not compulsory. You don't *have* to overdraw your account. It was still her own fault.)

Life is not always compassionate. There are hard lessons that must be learned. Don't balance your checkbook? You have only yourself to blame for overdrafts. Too much junk food and couch time? Only yourself to blame for poor health. Don't like school and won't go or study? Only yourself to blame for the meager job opportunities available to you. Too lazy or uncaring to tend to your appearance or practice personal hygiene? No wonder you don't have friends—only yourself to blame.

These are just some of the stark realities of life. You can learn them the hard way, or you can learn them from others who learned them the hard way and passed along lessons learned. In Proverbs and Ecclesiastes, Solomon candidly passes on the wisdom of life—wisdom he says he personally made it his aim to discover by experience (the hard way).

While Proverbs passes on nuggets of wisdom, Ecclesiastes does that *and* looks at the big picture. As you read it, underline the recurring phrase "under the sun" (twenty-seven times in twelve chapters). It means "in this life." What *should* be our main focus in *this* life?

The book flows as follows:

I)   A statement: None of life's normal pursuits are of lasting significance. 1:1–11

II) Solomon's experiments to see if that statement is true. He tries to find fulfillment in knowledge, fun, escape, work, personal purity, and philanthropy. None of these work. 1:12–2:26

III) On the other hand, he says, there is a time for everything in life. Live and find enjoyment in whatever moment God has given you, keeping in mind that one of those moments is an appointment with God to give an account for how you lived your life. 3:1–6:12

IV) Life is full of harsh realities. Face them wisely in full view of God. 7:1- 11:10

V)   Because old age (and the inability to make changes) and death is coming for us all, and then the judgment of God. 12:1- 14

Nothing we do, that stays here, "under the sun" is of lasting significance. What *is* of lasting significance is how we live in preparation for the time when we are no longer "under the sun," but in the presence of God. Jesus put it this way: "Do not store up for yourselves treasures on earth, where moth and rust destroy, and where thieves break in and steal. But store up for yourselves treasures in heaven, where moth and rust do not destroy, and where thieves do not break in and steal. For where your treasure is, there your heart will be also" (Matthew 6:19–21).

Song of Solomon

In the Hebrew Bible, the Song of Solomon is called the "Song of Songs" or "The best of songs." This book "celebrates the dignity and purity of human love . . . . It came to us in this world of sin, where lust and passion are on every hand, where fierce temptations assail us and try to turn us aside from the God-given standard of marriage. And it reminds us, in particularly beautiful fashion, how pure and noble love is" [G. Lloyd Carr, *The Song of Solomon* (Downers Grove, IL: IVP, 1984), 35].

The great love expressed in the Song of Solomon is between a man and his bride, in this case, Solomon, and a woman from the town of Shulam in northern Palestine. The book is presented very much like a play, divided into scenes.

Scene 1—The bride is brought to the chambers of the king's banqueting house. A chorus is sung by the "damsels of Jerusalem" and Solomon and the woman praise each other's beauty (1:1–2:8).

Scene 2—The bride's dream of her husband to be (2:9–3:5)

Scene 3—The marriage (3:6–5:10)

Scene 4—The marriage festival (5:2–8:4)

Scene 5—The couple visit the former home of the bride (8:5–14).

Historically, Christians have been somewhat reluctant to discuss the role of intimacy between men and women, but the Song of Solomon is a very intimate book. In an effort to avoid the issue, the book has been misinterpreted as referring to the love Jesus has for the church—this despite the fact that the book is not cited anywhere in the New Testament. Some of our hymns are based on this interpretation (e.g., "Jesus Rose of Sharon" and "I have Found a Friend in Jesus").

Four points are worth noting here about this book:

First, when it comes to couple relationships, sex is an important aspect. There's nothing wrong with that. It's the way God intended for things to work. But God has placed certain boundaries on sex. It is foolish for people to believe that couples forming and nurturing their relationships will not have sexual thoughts and feelings. The Song of Solomon reminds us that God has known this, planned it that way, and has spoken to the issue. Faithful people will pay attention to what God has said and keep within the boundaries of what God has said is proper.

Second, you will notice in the Song of Solomon that "looks" play an important role in the attraction between the sexes. It is important that after marriage both husband and wife understand that, and seek to remain attractive to their spouse.

Third, though looks are important, husbands and wives see one another differently from the way they see others. The woman of Shulam did not think she was as pretty or as cultured as the queens of Solomon's harem (1:5–6). But Solomon saw her with different eyes. In every successful marriage, the wife must know from her husband that he sees her differently from the way he sees other women—different even from the way she sees herself—and that he loves what he sees in her. The wife views her husband differently from the way she views other men, and she loves what she sees in him.

Finally, notice that Solomon and his bride communicate to each other their appreciation for one another. In modern relationships, pride often gets in the way of doing this, but successful marriages as God intended are relationships where husbands and wives continually communicate how they value each another, and they do so in positive ways.

Isaiah

Scholars often refer to the prophets as "covenant enforcement mediators." He was to remind God's people they were in an agreement with God. He was to remind them of what the agreement said. He was to rail against their disobedience, warn them of the consequences (that's where foretelling the future came in), and call them to change. I guess, when you think about it, his job was basically that of a preacher.

The *writing* prophets of the Old Testament are divided into "major prophets" and "minor prophets." "Major" and "minor" have only to do with the length of the books, not the importance of their content. There are four major prophets and twelve minor ones. The work of the writing prophets occurs after the division of God's people into a northern kingdom, Israel, and a southern one, Judah—about 900 BC. The longest of the major prophets is Isaiah and other than the Psalms, no book is cited or alluded to more often than this one.

Isaiah, a priest in Jerusalem, began his work during the final twenty years of the northern kingdom's history. During that time, Israel's greatest political threat was Assyria. Isaiah writes, however, not to Israel but to Judah. He uses Israel as an object lesson. For twenty years he will decry her wicked ways, urge her to turn to God, assure her of God's love for her, and warn her of the penalty for failure. When Isaiah's book is finished, the southern kingdom knows that what Isaiah has been saying to the north has been true. At that time, the south's great enemy is Babylon. Isaiah then turns his message to the south and, fundamentally, speaks the same thing to Judah.

Isaiah is divided into three parts.

I) Chapters 1–35 are poetry. They deal with the Assyrian threat and urge Israel to trust neither in her enemies nor her allies, but in God. There are three sections (1–12, 13–27, 28–35) and each ends with a poem of praise to God.

II) Chapters 36–39 are prose and tell the story of God's deliverance of his people from her enemies and emphasize the importance of trusting God.

III) Chapters 40–66 are poetry and are divided into three parts (40–48, 49–57, and 58–66), each ending with a warning of judgment against the wicked. The section emphasizes the great will of God to save those who will turn to him and his determination to judge those who will not.

Isaiah's relevance for the Christian Church has been largely limited to foretelling of the coming of Christ, and yet that is a minor concern for the prophet. He is supremely interested in God's people coming to trust in God. Those who will trust the Lord can be assured of God's favor and protection. Isaiah 25:6–9 is but a sample of many texts that could be cited to illustrate this point:

> On this mountain the LORD Almighty will prepare a feast of rich food for all peoples, a banquet of aged wine—the best of meats and the finest of wines. On this mountain he will destroy the shroud that enfolds all peoples, the sheet that covers all nations; he will swallow up death forever. The Sovereign LORD will wipe away the tears from all faces; he will remove the disgrace of his people from all the earth. The LORD has spoken. In that day they will say, "Surely this is our God;

we trusted in him, and he saved us. This is the LORD, we trusted in him; let us rejoice and be glad in his salvation." (See also Isaiah 28:16; 30:18; 40:29–31; 43:1–2; 49:13–23;65:24).

If Hebrews 11 is the great faith chapter in the Bible and Romans the great faith book of the New Testament, then surely Isaiah has to be the great faith book of the Old Testament.

Jeremiah and Lamentations

Jeremiah is one of the major prophets of the Old Testament. After God's people divided into two nations, the northern one continued until 722 BC. Isaiah is the major prophet of that time period. The southern kingdom continued until 586 BC Jeremiah was the major prophet of that period.

Jeremiah dates his work from the thirteenth year of King Josiah (627 BC).

In 609 BC, during a foolish war with Egypt, Josiah was killed and Judah lost her independence. He was succeeded by his son Jehoahaz. Egypt, however, as the conquering nation, felt they had the right to appoint a king of their own choosing, so they forcibly removed Jehoahaz and replaced him with Eliakim, another of Josiah's sons.

In 605 BC, the Babylonians conquered the Egyptians and carried away a number of the princes of Judah as spoils of war. Among them was Daniel, whose story is told in the Old Testament book that bears his name. In 597 BC, the Babylonians replaced Eliakim (whose other name is Jehoiakim) with Zedekiah. During all this time, Judah's greatest threat was from the Babylonians. She was tempted to ally herself with Egypt, but

Jeremiah knew her security lay in doing what she had never been able to do: submit to the will of God.

Jeremiah spoke out strongly against political corruption (5:4–5), oppression (7:6) and immorality. He condemned the men of Judah for acting like "well-fed, lusty stallions, each neighing after another man's wife" (5:8). He called Judah to submit to God's judgment against them for their sins, but his call was viewed as treason. His own people slandered him (18:18), beat him (20), threatened his life (26), threw him into prison (37) and down a well (38).

Jeremiah was a reluctant prophet. When God called Jonah to go to Nineveh, Jonah didn't object, he just didn't go. Jeremiah, however, complained. And yet he knew that the salvation of God's people depended on the work God had given him. He wrote: "Whenever I speak, I cry out proclaiming violence and destruction. So the word of the LORD has brought me insult and reproach all day long. But if I say, 'I will not mention him or speak any more in his name,' his word is in my heart like a fire, a fire shut up in my bones. I am weary of holding it in; indeed, I cannot" (20:8–9).

Jeremiah can be outlined as follows:

I) Jeremiah's call—chapter 1
II) Jeremiah calls Judah to repent—chapters 2–12
III) Punishment for sin predicted—chapters 13–29
IV) Promise of hope—chapters 30–35
V) Judah's fall—chapters 36–45
VI) Judgment against other nations—chapters 46–51
V) The Fall of Jerusalem—chapter 52.

Jeremiah's story and preaching was not just for Judah. God specifically says he was to be a prophet to the nations. The book serves as a reminder to all people, whether they are God's people or not, of the sovereignty of God. It is also a warning of judgment against all who would disregard the laws of God for living on the earth.

Jeremiah was the Old Testament suffering servant of the Lord. Jeremiah witnessed the destruction of his own people and his home town, and watched the bodies stack up like so much cord wood. He knew the people deserved the punishment they received, but their suffering pained him to the depths of his being. Jeremiah wrote: "Oh, that my head were a spring of water and my eyes a fountain of tears! I would weep day and night for the slain of my people" (9:1).

The phrase is repeated somewhat in Lamentations 1:16, and Lamentations is Jeremiah's suffering cry, a human reflection of the pain of God. I've officiated at funerals at Arlington National Cemetery several times and I can tell you, the playing of taps, usually by a bugler a little distance away, will stir the emotions whether you knew the deceased or not. When John F. Kennedy was buried, the grief of a nation impacted everyone gathered at the grave—including the bugler. The result was that he bungled the sixth note.

I mention this because the grief of Jeremiah (and God) in Lamentations comes through not only in his words, but in the book's structure. There are five poems. Four are twenty-two verses long. One is sixty-six verses long. They are supposed to be acrostics, each verse (or in the case of chapter three, each three verses) beginning with a successive letter in the twenty-two letter Hebrew alphabet. The first poem works fine. In the second, the poet stumbles, reversing the alphabet order in verses 16 and 17 and stumbles again in about the same place in chapters three and four. In chapter five, all composure is gone and though he sticks with twenty-two verses, the letter order is totally mixed up with some letters not represented at all. This is the mournful song of God for his children determined to go their own way.

Ezekiel

In your reading of Jeremiah, Ezekiel, and Daniel, two dates are important.

First, 605 BC. God had greatly reduced the size of his people by 605 BC, Israel, the Northern Kingdom, was no more, having fallen to an Assyrian occupation a little over a hundred years before. God had hoped the rest of his people, Judah, would get the point; he was serious about them paying attention to the covenant he had made with them.

They did not.

In 605 BC, Babylon went to war with Egypt and God's people were caught in the middle. Judah had sided with Egypt, and for that transgression, the King of Babylon defeated Judah as well, taking some of her princes as hostage back to Babylon. It wasn't just unfortunate happenstance. God had planned it. Among the hostages was Daniel, who wrote the book which bears his name. He wrote in Babylon, and his book is a reminder of how God rules over the nations of men and can bless His people no matter where they live.

Second, 597 BC. In that year Babylon once again went to war with Egypt, and once again, Judah sided with Egypt. This time, in defeating Egypt and Judah, the king of Babylon took hostage the King of Judah, replaced him with another, and took more hostages. Among them was Ezekiel.

Ezekiel, Daniel, and Jeremiah were all contemporaries.

Ezekiel was part of the imprisoned group of 597 BC. "As the LORD had declared, Nebuchadnezzar removed all the treasures from the temple of the LORD and from the royal palace, and took away all the gold articles that Solomon king of Israel had made for the temple of the LORD. He carried into exile all Jerusalem: all the officers and fighting men, and all the craftsmen and artisans--a total of ten thousand. Only the poorest people of the land were left" (2 Kings 24:13–14).

Those in captivity did not believe they would stay long. They earnestly believed they would be delivered and that the source of deliverance would be their kinsmen back home in Jerusalem. They believed their sins had separated them from God and his people and the Promised Land. Those left behind in Jerusalem must be the truly righteous, they thought, because *they* were not in captivity! In time, *they* would come rescue their brethren.

Ezekiel offers his readers in Babylon insight into what was truly going on in Jerusalem. If they were expecting deliverance from that quarter, they will be disappointed. The sins of Jerusalem's inhabitants are every bit as bad, and more so, than any they have committed. There will be no deliverance by them.

Ezekiel was a priest in the temple of God. Taken captive at age 30, he would have only just begun his priestly service. He speaks and writes to his countrymen who are exiled with him. Exile is not being homeless. "Rather, it is knowing that you do have a home, but that your home has been taken over by enemies." It is not being without roots. "On the contrary, it is having deep roots which have now been plucked up, and there you are, with roots dangling, writhing in pain, exposed to a cold and jeering world, longing to be restored to native and nurturing soil. Exile is knowing precisely where you belong, but knowing you can't go there—not yet. In exile, life cannot be "business as usual" (quotes from Ian Duguid, *The NIV Application Commentary: Ezekiel* (Grand Rapids, MI: Zondervan, 1999), 48).

The book is divided by dates into 13 sections. Watch for the date changes in your readings. They do not always signal a subject change, but they are good markers for your readings.

Ezekiel is important to us because Christians are also "in exile" (1 Peter 1:1, 17; 2:11). This world is not our home. We are looking for a better city, a city whose architect and builder is God. Ezekiel tells us how to live until we finally get to go home.

Daniel

Imagine! Imagine Osama Ben Laden stealing our Declaration of Independence from the National Archives and then burning it before our very eyes on an internet podcast.

Imagine our president, taken by force, from the White House, in handcuffs, to Baghdad, and the whole thing broadcast on the BBC.

Imagine whole families, thousands of people, uprooted from their homes and transported to Iran as slaves and hostages to ensure no reprisals.

Got it?

That's the picture of God's people in the late seventh century BC. The Babylonian king Nebuchadnezzar sent an army to Jerusalem, took their most sacred national treasures, and carried the king and the best and brightest of the Jewish empire as hostages to Babylon.

The captives had to wonder: "Where is God? Has the God of Israel met his match in the Babylonian empire?"

Among those captives were princes named Daniel, Hananiah, Mishael, and Azariah. Their story—and especially that of Daniel—is recounted in the book entitled Daniel.

The historical section of Daniel covers the period from 605 BC to 536 BC; the book appeared as a literary document after Judah's captivity, during the days when God's people were beginning to return to Jerusalem. The book has but one point: despite Israel's national shame and weakness, God, *their* God, was still God. No matter how it seemed at times, he still ruled over the kingdoms of this world and "gives them to anyone he wishes" (4:17).

Proof of God's sovereignty is offered in the first chapter as the author sets the stage for the main characters and places the reader in their world. These characters, though enslaved in a foreign country, rise inexplicably to positions of power—solely because God wills it (Daniel 1). In the second section, even the kings of Babylon and Persia come to understand that Israel's God is sovereign over them (2–7). In the final section of the book (8–12), Daniel receives visions for the future that illustrate the same thing. Years after Daniel's death and the circulation of this book, God's people, when they read Daniel, would take comfort in knowing that no matter how difficult the road, God was still taking care of them and would deliver them. Their assurance of the future rested on the demonstrations of God in their past.

Daniel remains important. Even though God's people are no longer defined at all by nationality or ethnicity, our God still rules over the nations and gives them to whomever he wishes, even the lowliest of people. Even though the nations of the world, have neither promise nor hope from God, they are still subject to him and they ignore him and his will at their own peril.

We, however, regardless of nationality, as followers of Jesus, are the People of God. No matter who holds public office, God sits on the throne. Our allegiance is solely to him; our hope rests exclusively in the one who rules as sovereign over all human kingdoms.

Hosea

The last twelve books of the Old Testament are called simply "The Twelve" or the Minor Prophets. They are *minor* not because they are unimportant, but because they are smaller than the other prophetical books. Keep in mind as you read them that the work of the prophet was not primarily to *foretell* the future, but to call God's people to *remember* their covenant with him, *remind* them of the blessings of that covenant, and *warn* them of the consequences of violating it.

The following minor prophets did their work during the period of the Divided Kingdom (when there was a Northern Kingdom, Israel, and a Southern Kingdom, Judah): Hosea, Joel, Amos, Jonah, and Nahum. The period covers the years 800–722 BC.

Obadiah, Micah, Habbakuk and Zephaniah did their work after the destruction of the Northern Kingdom, during the years 722–586 BC.

Judah, remember, was conquered and carried into Babylonian exile in 586 BC. She remained there until 539 BC when many of the captives were allowed to return to their homeland. Haggai, Zechariah, and Malachi did their work after 539 BC.

In the days before printing and Power Point, God sometimes used the life of a prophet to illustrate his message. Ezekiel was called to make a diorama of a besieged city outside his house and lie, tied up, on his side facing it, exposed to the elements for 390 days. The scene was to evoke the message of God's judgment on his people.

In the case of Hosea, God allowed him to marry Gomer, a woman whose background disposed her to unfaithfulness. True to her heritage, she cheated on him at every turn, bore three children—none of whom belonged to Hosea—and finally left Hosea to indulge her passions.

As always happens, however, her lovers eventually grew tired of her and finally, with no one who really cared about her, she was sold as a slave.

You have to wonder what Hosea's neighbors were saying about him—what a rotten deal he had gotten, how unfair it was that he was stuck caring for the children of his wife's adulteries. Hosea could have said: "Good riddance," found a wife who would love him, and gotten on with his life. But he didn't. Instead, he grieved over his lost love. Finally, he bought her out of slavery and brought her home.

Now imagine what the neighbors thought! Not only was his behavior beyond understanding, but they may have considered it a violation of God's law (Deuteronomy 24:1ff)!

But the story of Hosea and Gomer is the story of God and his people. His people were unfaithful to him beyond all excuse, but God loved them still and the story of God's enduring, persistent love, seen in the love of Hosea for Gomer, was intended to shame Israel into faithfulness.

The book can be outlined as follows:

I)   The story of Hosea and Gomer—chapters 1–3
II) Israel's unfaithfulness recounted—chapters 4–13
III) God's enduring love proclaimed—chapter 14

Joel

In 1915 a great locust plague devastated the entire region of the Holy Land from Egypt to the Taurus mountains in Turkey. The locusts came in February, darkening the sky as they flew and covering everything with their droppings. Within two months, every plant had been eaten and all the bark had been stripped from the trees. The locusts attacked people as well. Infant children, lacking the ability to knock off the locusts, had their exposed flesh eaten [story related in George I. Robinson, *The Twelve Minor Prophets* (Grand Rapids, MI: Baker, 1926), 33].

It was the fourth plague to strike the area in 23 years, and just one of many locust plagues history records in the area. One of those recordings is contained in the "minor prophet" book of Joel. Joel was likely written during the time of the divided kingdom of Israel, probably in the eighth century BC. He describes the plague like this: "Has not the food been cut off before our very eyes—joy and gladness from the house of our God? The seeds are shriveled beneath the clods. The storehouses are in ruins, the granaries have been broken down, for the grain has dried up. How the cattle moan! The herds mill about because they have no pasture; even the flocks of sheep are suffering" (Joel 1:16).

Joel wrote specifically for the southern kingdom of Judah, saying to them: "If you think this locust plague was bad, you haven't seen anything yet" (2:2). Because of Judah's sinfulness, God promised to send a foreign army on his own people to subdue and punish them. The army, and the devastation in its wake, would be worse than a plague of locusts.

Joel does not present a catalog of Judah's sins. Only drunkenness is specifically mentioned. But as you read through the book, God seems upset about two things. First, people simply do not give God much thought. The priests perform their duties in the temple, but those are more ritual than deep heartfelt service to God in behalf of the people. The people have gotten on with their lives with little thought about what God wants *for* them, and even less thought about what God wants *of* them. Second, God is upset at their lack of offerings to him.

But the calamity of the locust plague has brought normal life to an end. Now, Joel writes, is the time to think about your lives and make God a part of them. "'Even now,' declares the LORD, 'return to me with all your heart, with fasting and weeping and mourning. Rend your heart and not your garments. Return to the LORD your God, for he is gracious and compassionate, slow to anger and abounding in love, and he relents from sending calamity. Who knows? He may turn and have pity and leave behind a blessing-- grain offerings and drink offerings for the LORD your God'" (2:12–14). The plague has come because the people have not thought about God enough to make offerings to him. He has responded by taking away everything they have so that no offerings are possible. When they return to him, he will bless them once more.

The "day of the Lord" is a signature phrase for Joel. It is a day of judgment. For those who have persecuted God's people, it will be a day of desolation. For the unfaithful of God's people, it will be a day of devastation. But for those who are faithful, it will be a day of shelter and blessing accompanied by the presence of God's Spirit.

We can divide Joel as follows:

I)   The locust plague recounted—chapter 1
II) Promised punishment from God and a call to
     repentance—chapter 2:1–17

III) The judgment of God—chapters 2:18–3:21

We are normally reluctant to attribute natural calamity to God. "God doesn't send earthquakes or famines or war," we contend. As a result, when these things happen, we seldom think of God. Old Testament people believed God was behind all things, and that God used those things to get the attention of those he loved. Because of our approach, it's harder for God to get our attention, and the constant danger is that we will end up just like the people who first received the book of Joel.

Amos

At the death of Solomon, about 931 BC, his kingdom was torn in two and became known as the kingdoms of Israel (in the north) and Judah (in the south). Jeroboam, a descendant of Joseph, became Israel's first king. Jeroboam was chosen by God for this position and had God's blessing; but Jeroboam faithlessly (and stupidly) chose to rebel against God, installing worship centers in the cities of Dan and Bethel, all in an effort to solidify a monarchy already guaranteed by God. He set up golden idols at those sites and encouraged the people to worship them. They did, and very soon afterward God made their lives incredibly difficult by sending the Syrians and the Assyrians to oppress them. From 805–735 BC, however, there was a break in the oppression and Israel began to prosper. But rather than turn to God in repentance, Israel drew further away.

It was during this time that God sent a poor man from Tekoa (12 miles south of Jerusalem) to preach to them. His task was to get Israel to repent and warn them of the consequences of impenitence. His name was Amos, and his message to Israel was simple and ominous: "Prepare to meet your God" (4:12).

The book of Amos begins (1–2) somewhat deceptively in that it addresses the sins of the nations surrounding Israel. Hearing this, Amos' audience and readers could not help but believe that they were God's favored nation.

But beginning in chapter 3, and extending virtually to the end of the book (9:10), the prophet condemns, in the harshest language, the sins of Israel. He describes the rich women of Israel as "cows of Bashan." He accuses Israel of turning justice into bitterness and "throwing righteousness to the ground." He condemns their lives of indolence with these words: "You lie on beds inlaid with ivory and lounge on your couches. You dine on choice lambs and fattened calves. You strum away on your harps like David . . . You drink wine by the bowlful and use the finest lotions, but you do not grieve over the ruin of Joseph" (6:4–6).

God's mighty hand of judgment looms and there will be no escape. "Not one will get away; none will escape. Though they dig down to the depths of the grave, from there my hand will take them. Though they hide themselves on the top of Carmel, there I will hunt them down and seize them. . . . Though they are driven into exile by their enemies, there will I command the sword to slay them. I will fix my eyes on them for evil and not for good" (9:1–4).

Israel's sins all spring from their blessings: they are all out to "get theirs" and they will oppress all who get in their way. They despise authority and correction and love to revel in the finest the world has to offer. But they have no time for God and no time for the needy. Such a people, in the eyes of God, do not deserve to live.

God will not, however, do away with them all. They are, after all, God's people. And so, after a time of great trial and destruction, God promises to restore his people and show the world that, while subject to his justice, they are not subject to obliteration (9:11–15). This latter text is cited in the New Testament to refer to the Christian church (Acts 15:16–17).

How do we apply this book? After all, it is addressed to the nation of Israel, not to *our* nation.

On one hand, we cannot say that, if our nation practices the same sins of Israel, we will fall as she did. Our nation does not, as a nation, sustain the same relationship to God that Israel did nor is it the beneficiary of God's promises. The people of God, today, are Christians in every nation. The message of Amos is that God is serious about justice and mercy and fairness and true spirituality. If we buy into the value system of the world, we will suffer the adverse judgment of God no matter what our nationality might be.

On the other hand, the beginning of Amos makes plain that God holds all nations accountable for the way they conduct themselves. Failure to pay attention to God's standard of conduct will surely usher in an earlier demise. It is in the best interests of the world for Christians, in whatever nation they reside, to live and promote the ways of God, both for our own future and for the benefit of those among whom we live.

Obadiah

Abraham had two sons, Ishmael and Isaac. Isaac had two sons, Jacob and Esau. Jacob became the father of the Israelite nation. Esau became the father of the Edomite nation. Jacob, the younger of the two, stole his brother's inheritance. Years later, when all seemed forgiven, Jacob lied to his brother. No matter what the reasons or whose fault the feud was, God forbade Jacob's descendants, Israel, to mistreat her brethren the Edomites.

When Israel left Egypt during the Exodus, the old animosity between the two families arose. Israel asked to pass through Edomite territory on the king's highway, promising not to "go through any field or vineyard, or drink water from any well. We will travel along the king's highway and not turn to the right or to the left until we have passed through your territory. If we or our livestock drink any of your water, we will pay for it. We only want to pass through on foot—nothing else." Edom replied, "You may not pass through here; if you try, we will march out and attack you with the sword" (cf. Numbers 20:14–20).

Edom never forgave Israel. The nation remembered every perceived slight and never forgot an insult. Amos wrote: Edom "pursued his brother with a sword, stifling all compassion, because his anger raged continually, and his fury flamed unchecked" (Amos 1:11).

When Israel was conquered and Jerusalem burned by the Babylonians, the Edomites surveyed the situation from a distance, celebrating the defeat of her brethren. Obadiah recounts this scene in the book that bears his name, and delivers God's promise of destruction for Edom's treatment of Israel.

Two points should not be lost on the people of God: First, we must be forgiving. We are not allowed to hold a grudge and the severest punishment awaits those who do. Second, God has not ordained any particular government or any system of government as his anointed on the earth. Nor are God's people defined by particular political boundaries or philosophies. No government or system of government on the earth is eternal. They are *all* temporary, subject to the sovereignty of God. Obadiah reminds us that the longevity of every nation depends on the attitudes and actions of its people, and those nations whose citizens find it hard to forgive and who rejoice in the misfortunes of others are nations destined to be short-lived.

Jonah

Jonah is likely the best known minor prophet—the prophet who got swallowed by the whale (or "big fish," depending on your translation). Could a fish swallow a man whole and the man survive? After three days in a whale's belly? I've wondered what the inside of a whale's belly looks like. Jonah probably couldn't tell us since there would have been no light. What would it smell like?

When you begin to focus on the story, I can't imagine anything more horrible than Jonah's condition, a situation much akin to being buried alive. In fact, that's how Jonah described it: "From the depths of the grave I called for help . . . . The engulfing waters threatened me, the deep surrounded me; seaweed was wrapped around my head . . . my life was ebbing away" (Jonah 2:1, 5, 7).

But actually the book of Jonah is not primarily about Jonah at all. It is a book about God.

Jonah lived during the days of Jeroboam II in the northern kingdom of Israel. Though times were prosperous, political disaster lay just over the horizon. The world power was the Assyrian nation, and the world had seldom seen such power wielded with such cruelty. Their kings bragged about slaughtering their enemies and dying the mountains red like wool with their blood, burning young men and maidens alive, and covering the walls of conquered cities and the columns of local buildings with the skins of beaten people. Not surprisingly, no one liked the Assyrians.

And so, when God told the prophet Jonah to go preach to the Assyrians and tell them to turn from their wicked ways, or else, Jonah thought "or else" suited them just fine. Rather than make the 500 mile trek to Nineveh, Jonah caught a ship headed in the opposite direction for Spain.

That's when "the weather started getting rough." In an ocean storm, there are no atheists. Every passenger prayed to his god and when Jonah confessed that he was the reason for the storm, the passengers prayed to Jonah's God—then threw Jonah overboard. The sea grew calm—just as Jonah told them it would. God caused the big fish to swallow Jonah, and Jonah went to "time out." It was there that Jonah realized that when God gives you a job, it's easier to do it than refuse. Jonah repented, and the fish "vomited Jonah onto dry land."

Jonah then went to preach to the Assyrians. They listened, turned from their wickedness, and Jonah got angry. He knew it would happen. The Assyrians would survive when, in Jonah's mind, they deserved to die. In a fit of pique, he camped outside the city of Nineveh and pouted.

This is where you get to the point of the story.

God caused a plant to grow overnight to shade Jonah. Then, just as quickly, God killed it. Jonah, no longer sheltered from the sun, became furious. At that point God sat Jonah down for a heart to heart. Jonah was angry because a plant he had neither planted nor cultivated had died. God said: "Shouldn't I be concerned for a city filled with innocent children and cattle?"

Jonah is full of wonderful lessons. God loves all people. His people may be the people of blessing and promise, but he still loves everyone. Second, God expects all people (whether his or not) to submit to his will. Third, those who don't will find life exceedingly hard. But most of all, he is a God of grace and forgiveness. The people of Nineveh experienced it. So did Jonah. Fourth, God expects his people to speak to the people of the world to reveal his will.

Micah

In the final days of Judah, the prophet Jeremiah issued a stinging rebuke to the nation in the holy city of Jerusalem: "This is what the LORD says: If you do not listen to me and follow my law, which I have set before you, and if you do not listen to the words of my servants the prophets, whom I have sent to you again and again (though you have not listened), then I will make this house like Shiloh and this city an object of cursing among all the nations of the earth" (Jeremiah 26:4–6).

For hundreds of years before Solomon, the city of Shiloh had been the home of the Tabernacle and the presence of God. But Israel had been disobedient, believing that God's presence would insure them against catastrophe regardless of how they lived. At one point they even carried the Ark of the Covenant into battle, believing its presence guaranteed victory.

The ark was captured. Shiloh was destroyed.

Now Jeremiah was telling them the same thing would happen to Jerusalem if it's citizens didn't mend their ways.

The religious elite of Jerusalem arrested Jeremiah and brought him to court, charging: "This man should be sentenced to death because he has prophesied against this city. You have heard it with your own ears!" Jeremiah, in their eyes, was guilty of treason.

Fortunately, some of the older, respected men of the community stepped forward in Jeremiah's behalf. They said: "Micah of Moresheth in the days of King Hezekiah said: 'Zion will be plowed like a field, Jerusalem will become a heap of rubble, the temple hill a mound overgrown with thickets.' No one put Micah to death. Instead, they repented."

And so Jeremiah's life was spared—thanks to the work of Micah. Unlike the days of Micah, however, the people didn't repent.

The prophecy of Micah is found in the book that bears his name. He did his work about the middle of the eighth century BC, just before the fall of the Northern Kingdom. His book describes the people of God in a most unflattering manner. They "lay awake at night plotting treachery against their neighbors." They use their power to oppress people—just because they can. They "hate good and love evil" (3:2). They will do anything to make a dollar. Their lack of concern for others is vividly portrayed in these words addressed to the political leaders: "[Y]ou tear the skin from my people . . . break their bones in pieces . . . [and] chop them up like meat for the pan, like flesh for the pot" (3:3). Religious leaders led Israel astray, preaching an "I'm okay, you're okay gospel," and they did it because that was precisely what the people wanted to hear. In God's mind, his church had been ruined "beyond all remedy."

The result? "Zion will be plowed like a field, Jerusalem will become a heap of rubble, the temple hill a mound overgrown with thickets" (3:12). It didn't happen immediately of course. Jeremiah was still talking about the coming calamity two hundred years after Micah. But less than twenty years later, the end had come—just as God said.

What did God want from his people? Simply this: "to act justly and to love mercy and to walk humbly with God" (Micah 6:8). If they would but do that, God would pardon and forgive them, hurling their sins into "the depths of the sea" (Micah 7:19).

Micah stands as a lasting rebuke to the people of God in every age who, remembering who they are, forget what they are about; people who, because of their relationship with God, believe they can get away with being inattentive to his will. Micah also has a message for the world: God is sovereign over the nations. They may deny his existence and repudiate his will, but God remains sovereign, and ultimately he promises to "take vengeance in anger and wrath upon the nations that have not obeyed me" (Micah 5:14–15).

Micah affirms that God delights to show mercy (7:18), but is unafraid to discipline the wayward.

Nahum

Likely the best known of all the Minor Prophets is the book of Jonah. Jonah was a prophet of the eighth century BC during the reign of Jeroboam II; God called him to preach to the Assyrian nation to turn them from their wicked ways. Jonah was successful, the Assyrians repented, and calamity was averted.

For a while.

But it didn't take long for the Assyrians to return to their wicked ways, and when they did, they returned with a vengeance. Old Testament scholar Jack Lewis writes of the Assyrian nation: "Assyria . . . was a nation largely geared for aggressive war. Its atrocities were proverbial as the records and art left by its kings make quite clear. . . . Its victims lay prone under its tyranny . . . . Nineveh saw men and nations as tools to be exploited to gratify the lust of conquest and commercialism. Assyria existed to render no service to mankind" [Jack P. Lewis, *Minor Prophets* (Austin, TX: Sweet, 1966), 43].

Assyria attacked and destroyed the northern kingdom of Israel less than fifty years after the time of Jonah. The southern kingdom of Judah also felt her cruelty at the hands of Assyrian kings Sargon II and Sennacherib (721–681 BC). Hezekiah foolishly tried to make a stand against Assyria and, had it not been for God's intervention, would have lost his kingdom. The chutzpah of the kings of Assyria is most clearly heard in these words of an Assyrian field commander to the besieged people of Judah: "Do not let Hezekiah deceive you, for he shall not be able to deliver you from [my] hand; nor let Hezekiah make you trust in the Lord, saying, 'The Lord will surely deliver us; this city shall not be given into the hand of the king of Assyria. . . . Do not listen to Hezekiah . . . . Has the god of any nation ever delivered his land from the hand of the king of Assyria? . . . . Who of all the gods of these countries has been able to save his land from me? How then can the Lord deliver Jerusalem from my hand?'" (2 Kings 18:32–35).

At this point, God had had enough. The Lord struck 185,000 Assyrian soldiers dead in one night; about this time the prophet Nahum appeared on the scene to announce to Judah Assyria's end. "Trouble," the prophet assured them, at least from Assyria, "will not come a second time" (1:9).

Nahum proclaims the absolute sovereignty of God: "He makes all the rivers run dry. . . . The mountains quake before him and the hills melt away. The earth trembles at his presence, the world and all who live in it" (1:5). Though he is slow to anger, a refuge in times of trouble and cares for all who trust in him, you don't want to make him angry. "Who can withstand his indignation? Who can endure his fierce anger? His wrath is poured out like fire; the rocks are shattered before him" (1:6–7). In no uncertain terms, the nation of Assyria stood condemned before God. "I will prepare your grave," God says, "for you are vile" (1:14). "'I am against you,' declares the LORD Almighty. 'I will burn up your chariots in smoke, and the sword will devour your young lions' [or princes]. 'I will leave you no prey on the earth. The voices of your messengers will no longer be heard'" (2:13).

Nahum catalogs Assyria's sins. She is cruel, unprincipled, immoral, and dedicated to one thing: increasing profits for her merchants whose number rivals the stars of the sky. But her end is assured: "Nothing can heal your wound," God says: "your injury is fatal." No one will mourn her passing: "Everyone who hears the news about you claps his hands at your fall, for who has not felt your endless cruelty?" (3:19).

Less than fifty years after Nahum, Nineveh, the capital city of Assyria, and the empire itself, fell under the onslaught of the Babylonians, Medes, and the Scythians (612 BC). Jack Lewis writes: "The destruction was so complete that when Xenophon and his 10,000 Greeks passed by the site 200 years later, they gave no indication of knowing that the capital had existed" (Lewis, *Minor Prophets*, 43).

All nations, including our own, exist by permission and design of God, and no nation, indifferent to the will of God, exists for long. If Nahum teaches us anything, it is that those nations playing fast and loose with God's rules of justice, fairness, compassion, and ethics will come to a short, certain, devastating and ignominious end.

Habakkuk

Throughout the Bible many have questioned God—and not just for information. When the Lord declared his intention to destroy the cities of Sodom and Gomorrah, Abraham replied: "Will you sweep away the righteous with the wicked? What if there are fifty righteous people in the city? Will you really sweep it away and not spare the place for the sake of the fifty righteous people in it? . . . . Will not the Judge of all the earth do right?" (Genesis 18:23ff).

During the Exodus, Israel complained to Moses, and Moses complained to God: "Did I conceive all these people? Did I give them birth? Why do you tell me to carry them in my arms, as a nurse carries an infant, to the land you promised on oath to their forefathers? . . . . They keep wailing to me, ... I cannot carry all these people by myself; the burden is too heavy for me. If this is how you are going to treat me, put me to death right now . . ." (Numbers 11:12).

Facing oppression, the sons of Korah cried out to God "Awake, O Lord! Why do you sleep? Rouse yourself! Do not reject us forever. Why do you hide your face and forget our misery and oppression?" (Psalm 44:23–24).

These are not the only examples. The list of God's interrogators is not a short one.

As long as Judah had Israel to compare herself to, it was easy to overlook her own sins. But after the destruction of the Northern Kingdom, Judah was left to contemplate her own situation. Other prophets decried the injustice and materialism of Judah. At this time, however, Habakkuk arose, not to condemn his people, but to ask God why *he* wasn't condemning them. "How long, O LORD, must I call for help, but you do not listen?

Or cry out to you, 'Violence!' but you do not save? Why do you make me look at injustice? Why do you tolerate wrong?"

God replied (Habakkuk 1) that he was going to punish Judah by bringing against her the Babylonians, "that ruthless and impetuous people, who sweep across the whole earth to seize dwelling places not their own."

This put a whole new twist on things. The Babylonians!? Why in the world would God punish Judah with people *worse* than Judah? Habakkuk was indignant. "I will stand at my watch," he wrote, "and station myself on the ramparts; I will look to see what he will say to me . . . ." It was unjust of God, Habakkuk thought, for God to use sinners worse than Judah to punish Judah. Frankly, Habakkuk believed God had gotten himself in a moral bind on this one and Habakkuk was determined to hold God accountable.

In a lengthy reply (chapter two), God speaks to the arrogance of Habakkuk, which is very much like the arrogance of Judah and Babylon. Habakkuk is a product of his times. God affirms that he will hold both Babylon and Judah responsible for their sins. No one is getting a pass. The Lord ends his speech with a proclamation of his sovereignty.

Habakkuk, properly rebuked, spends chapter three of his book in prayer. He reviews God's power, but also God's faithfulness to his people. Habakkuk understands that Judah must be punished for her sins. He knows the punishment will be inevitable. No matter who does it, however, God will not desert his people, and in that Habakkuk can find hope. "I heard and my heart pounded, my lips quivered at the sound; decay crept into my bones, and my legs trembled. Yet I will wait patiently for the day of calamity to come on the nation invading us. Though the fig tree does not bud and there are no grapes on the vines, though the olive crop fails and the fields produce no food, though there are no sheep in the pen and no cattle in the stalls, yet I will rejoice in the LORD, I will be joyful in God my Savior" (3:16–18).

God has no problem with his people questioning him, or even disagreeing with him. But he insists that, at the end of the day, the people trust him. He is God. We are not. Those who stand "right" in the sight of God are those who, in the end, trust God and demonstrate it with the life they live. Being "right" with God is supremely a matter of trusting God. This very important point is made in 2:4. Paul quotes this text in Romans (1:17) and Galatians (3:11) to reaffirm that same point to his own readers.

Zephaniah

Do you have a relative who is a "thorn in your side"? No? King Josiah did. The relative's name was Zephaniah. He is the only prophet (except perhaps for Daniel) of royal blood—the great-great-grandson of King Hezekiah.

Josiah's grandfather was Manasseh, the worst king in Judah's history. He promoted the worship of idols and the assimilation of other religions into the religion of Israel. He burned one of his sons as a sacrifice to a pagan deity and enacted oppressive policies that resulted in the wholesale slaughter of all who opposed him. His corrupt monarchy led Judah into evil worse than any of the nations around her, in her own day or before. So evil was he that the writer of Kings blames him for Judah's misfortunes and ultimately Babylonian exile (2 Kings 23:26).

Josiah, however, was not evil. At age 26 he began a series of reforms in Judah to lead the people back to God. It was a valiant effort, but in God's eyes, and the eyes of Josiah's cousin Zephaniah, it was too little too late. Judah was too far gone.

It must have been a source of great consternation to Josiah that, though he wanted his people to change their ways, his own royal house and the house of the priests was so corrupt that his efforts were like putting out a forest fire with a garden hose. It must have brought further discouragement to hear the negative message preached by Zephaniah.

By Zephaniah's day, the Northern Kingdom was no more. Judah's sins were so many that the anger of God overflowed. It's almost as if God was on a rampage, his anger spilling out (though deservedly so) on other nations. Notice God's determination: "I will sweep away everything from the face of the earth . . ." (1:2). "I will bring distress on the people . . . . their blood will be poured out like dust and their entrails like filth" (1:17). "In the fire of his jealousy the whole world will be consumed, for he will make a sudden end of all who live on the earth . . ." (1:18). "The whole world will be consumed by the fire of my jealous anger" (3:8).

What were the sins? Idolatry (1:4), ignoring God (1:6), becoming too much like the world around them in their dress and lifestyle (1:8–9), focusing on material wealth and a willingness to mistreat others to get it (1:11–13, 18), a belief that God simply didn't care how they acted (1:12), and a ruinous unwillingness to yield to God (3:1–4).

God repeatedly says he is going to destroy the earth and everything and everyone; and yet, God speaks of a "remnant" who will be left. It is a classic overstatement—and that's how the book is to be read. Overstatement or not, however, a genuine day of reckoning is coming and it will be ruinous for the guilty.

Zephaniah has four parts:

I) The coming punishment of the people of God
(1:1–2:3)

II) The coming punishment of other nations (2:4–15)

III) The coming punishment of the people of God
(3:1–8)

IV) The restoration of the remnant of God's people
(3:9–20)

Two points should not be overlooked: First, note that both the people of God and other nations stand condemned for precisely the same sins. God does not have two standards of expected behavior. The world may not acknowledge God, but God expects them none-the-less to follow his rules. Second, though God is supremely angry in Zephaniah, he still loves his people. When the punishment is over, God will take great delight in the righteous who are left; he will quiet them with his love and rejoice over them with singing (3:17)—the image of a parent reaffirming love for a disciplined child.

There is a message here for us as we face our own day of reckoning. Zephaniah is not quoted in the New Testament, but in the judgment day scene of Revelation 10:7, I cannot help but believe that the writer at least had Zephaniah in mind: "But in the days when the seventh angel is about to sound his trumpet, the mystery of God will be accomplished, just as he announced to his servants the prophets" (Revelation 10:7).

Haggai

The end began in 605 BC, as the military might of Babylon challenged that of Egypt and Judah, the remnant of the people of God, was squeezed in the middle. Many of her nobility were carted off as prisoners of Nebuchadnezzar, hostages to peace. Babylon exerted her might again in 597 BC, and finally in 586. In the end, Jerusalem lay in ruins, an empty, ghastly shell of her former self. Her wall lay on its side and her temple, the dream of David, was looted and burned. The once glorious Zion of God had been both witness and victim of some of the worst atrocities of human history.

God was responsible, but Judah was to blame. Even then, in the eyes of God, she'd received far less than her due.

But God's grace abounded. In 539 BC, Cyrus, king of the Persians gave permission for the exiles to return to Jerusalem to rebuild—a fulfillment of the specific promises of God through Isaiah (300 years before) and Jeremiah (nearly 100 years before). And if that were not evidence enough of God's grace, Ezra tells us they returned as they had left Egypt—unexpectedly prosperous. Some fifty thousand returned in the first wave and within a year they set about rebuilding the house of God.

It was an exciting time.

But after a while the new wore off. They encountered opposition from the people around them. The squatters didn't like Judah returning to reclaim what the neighbors had appropriated for themselves. They'd rejoiced in the Jews' misfortune, and they weren't about to let them rebuild a nation they had so delightedly seen destroyed.

The people of God gave in and gave up. The temple foundation was as far as they got. After all, they had themselves to think about. When they had re-established themselves in the land, *then* they would see about rebuilding God's house.

Nearly twenty years passed. Twenty years without the worship of God at the temple. Twenty years of trying to be the people of God without the proper worship of God. The important gave way to the tyranny of the urgent and success eluded them all. In 520 BC, God sent two prophets, Haggai and Zechariah, to demand that God be given the proper place in their lives.

In Haggai, God tells the people that their "never being able to get ahead" was their own fault. They had not put God first. "This is what the LORD Almighty says: 'Give careful thought to your ways. You have planted much, but have harvested little. You eat, but never have enough. You drink, but never have your fill. You put on clothes, but are not warm. You earn wages, only to put them in a purse with holes in it. . . . You expected much, but see, it turned out to be little. What you brought home, I blew away. Why?' declares the LORD Almighty. 'Because of my house, which remains a ruin, while each of you is busy with his own house'" (Haggai 1:9).

In a series of four speeches, all dated and providing an outline for Haggai, the prophet called Judah to repentance. The real surprise was that Judah really did repent. Construction was restarted and within four years the temple was finished.

Haggai also makes it plain that rebuilding the temple was not Judah's only problem. The lifestyle of the people fell far below any threshold for holiness. Continuing in that path would result in more frustration as God refused to allow them to succeed materially.

Does Haggai speak to our time?

Yes, in at least this way: God's temple today is not a building of stone and mortar, but a building of living stones, the church. When we get to wondering why we work so hard and never seem to be able to "pull ahead," it's worth asking whether our lives are demonstrating that God is our first priority. The answer won't always be "no." But if it is, repentance is in order. Our task is to build up the church by being involved in the community of faith to strengthen one another and draw outsiders in. Failing to give God the priority he deserves by giving attention to his church follows in the footsteps of the returning exiles. Success will be elusive. God will be responsible, but the fault will be our own.

Zechariah

In my view, Zechariah is the most challenging of the Minor Prophets. Its difficulty lies in its uniqueness. It is not written like anything within our normal experience. It is full of visions (which require interpretation) and oracles which, frankly, are supposed to be different from the rest of the book but just sound the same.

And yet, in the gospel story of the end of Jesus' life, Zechariah is the most cited literature of the Bible. Ancient people loved it.

Ezra tells us that about the year 520 BC, Haggai and Zechariah, two prophets of the Lord, rose up and encouraged the people to complete the temple. Haggai offers God's criticism against Judah for improper priorities: they've given attention to every worldly thing and not a moment's consideration to God. The command of the Lord is plain: "Get the temple rebuilt."

Zechariah likewise calls on the people to rebuild the temple, but mostly his is an assurance that the temple *will* be rebuilt. It will involve the efforts of God's people, but it will be accomplished by his power. This was to be an encouragement to Judah.

A month before Zechariah began his work, God had promised through Haggai to upset the nations around Judah and cause her to be admired and exalted. It was a huge promise. A month later, nothing had happened. There were plenty in Judah wondering if God's promises weren't just false hopes on their part. Zechariah focuses on the assurance that the promises of God will be fulfilled.

Haggai is divided by the dates the author references for the messages he receives. Zechariah also has dates, but his book is arranged more by the different ways he presents his message. It can be divided into seven parts as follows:

1) Dated the eighth month of Darius' second year, the prophet assures the people that God's words have always come true. Nothing has changed. 1:1–6

2) Eight visions emphasize that
   a) God knows what is going on in the world and with his people. He is determined to bless his own (first vision—1:7–17).
   b) God intends to punish those who have made life so miserable for his people (second vision 1:18–21).
   c) Jerusalem will be rebuilt and it will be glorious (third vision 2:1–10).
   d) God's forgiveness and cleansing is promised (fourth vision 3:1–10).
   e) God himself will accomplish this (fifth vision 4:1–14)
   f) Sin is condemned (sixth vision 5:1–4).
   g) Sin is banished (seventh vision 5:5–11).
   h) Peace will come to the people of God (eighth vision 6:1–8).

3) The prophet Zechariah is involved in an object lesson that unites the monarchy and priesthood of Judah (7:1–14).

4) Dated the fourth day of the ninth month of Darius' fourth year, God emphasizes his determination to bless his people (7:1–8:23).
5) An "oracle" (9:1–11:3) again promises blessing to the people of God.
6) An object lesson calls all of God's people, especially their leaders, to turn from sin (11:4–17).
7) An "oracle" (12:1–14:21) describes the blessed kingdom of God's people.

There are five emphases in Zechariah:

- First, God does know what is going on in the world, because he is making it happen.
- Second, God has a special regard for those who are his, and has marvelous plans for them.
- Third, the blessings are contingent upon God's people conforming their lives to his directives. Zechariah gives an excellent summary of this lifestyle in 7:9–10 and in 8:16–19.
- Fourth, no one, absolutely no one, will disrespect God and get away with it.
- Finally, God's dream is for all the people of the world to unite under his guidance and give him the glory he deserves.

Zechariah may be a little more difficult to read than the other Minor Prophets, but it is immensely relevant nonetheless.

Malachi

Malachi is the final book of the Old Testament in our English Bibles. In the Hebrew Bible, it is the concluding book of the prophets. One way or another, Malachi has a final say.

Unlike most of the prophets, nothing in Malachi gives us a clue to its date. There are echoes here of Isaiah, Jeremiah, and Zechariah—particularly in the use of the name for God: "Lord Almighty"—which leads us to our main observation about the book: It is the message of a deeply offended God.

In Malachi, God is offended because of the things his people have said:

- God doesn't love us.
- The rituals of our religion are beneath us: We don't like that "old time religion" of our forefathers.
- There is no "one way," no right or wrong.
- God won't do anything to us, good or bad.
- Serving God isn't to our advantage.

In Malachi God is offended because his people have not treated him with honor. He is the Lord Almighty, whose name is great from one end of the world to another. He is the "great king" whose name is to be feared and respected. And yet Israel has not treated him with the deference he deserves. They offer sacrifices not even the governor of the land would accept as a gift. God calls them a bunch of "cheats." They mistreat their wives. They engage in violence, sexual immorality, and oppression of the poor. It is, to God, amazing that his people, knowing him, could act in such reprehensible ways and not be quaking with fear at the retribution they know their behavior deserves and will receive.

Malachi promises a day of reckoning. A messenger from the Lord will come to herald the arrival of God himself. It will not, according to Malachi, be a welcome sight.

Malachi also promises a day of blessing, but before it comes, the lives of his people must change: "the hearts of the fathers must turn to their children." If they don't, the day of blessing will be a day of cursing.

The arrival of John the Baptist, the forerunner of Jesus, is often cited in the New Testament as a fulfillment of God's promises through Malachi, but that is surely not all the book is about. It speaks of honoring God with our lives and in our worship; and, the prophet focuses on our giving to the Lord as an example of how to show honor.

Giving to God is not charity. Giving to God is not showing our support for worthy causes. Giving to God is a means of demonstrating respect toward the Lord. In the Old Testament, God's people were required to appear before him in assembly three times a year. On all three occasions, the Lord says, "Don't show up without a gift" (Deuteronomy 16:16). The gift was a demonstration of honor (remember the wise men bringing gifts to the baby Jesus?). The gift was also a demonstration of trust in God's ability and willingness to take care of his people. The Lord says: "Bring the whole tithe into the storehouse, that there may be food in my house. Test me in this," says the LORD Almighty, "and see if I will not throw open the floodgates of heaven and pour out so much blessing that you will not have room enough for it" (Malachi 3:10).

As the people of God, we cannot divorce the *way* we live from our relationship with God. If we live sorry lives that evidence dishonor, as people of God or not, we stand "cursed" by the Lord.

Malachi ends and the voice of God is quiet. It will stay quiet for four hundred years until the messenger of God proclaims the coming of Jesus. But the message of Malachi is for all time: God is watching and listening. He longs to bless, but is far too often offended. A final trumpet will sound and a day of reckoning will arrive just as God "announced to his servants the prophets" (Revelation 10:7). Are you ready?

7

Books of the Bible— New Testament

Matthew

Matthew was one of Jesus' inner circle of friends he called "apostles." His other name was Levi. Matthew was a tax collector, an occupation despised by the Jewish orthodoxy for two reasons: the offices were filled with corruption, and the taxes went to a hated government, Rome. No self-respecting orthodox Jew would have anything to do with tax-collectors. They regarded them as no better than drunkards. Perhaps because of this, Matthew, in his Gospel, seems to take great pride that Jesus, despite Matthew's occupation, would call him to be a disciple.

From the second century until very near our own time, Christians regarded Matthew as the most important Gospel. Matthew was an eyewitness to Jesus' ministry, Luke was not, and Mark was considered an abbreviated version of Matthew.

Matthew was written for Christians. They lived in the city and likely were people of means (Matthew mentions money more than all the other Gospel writers together). But their prosperity could not save them from difficult times, even persecution. Matthew mentions trials and persecutions more than any other Gospel writer. Rather than say "keep on going, these difficult days cannot last forever," Matthew points his readers beyond this earth and our time frame to the day when all suffering for God's people will end and they join Jesus with God in heaven. And so, when Matthew wrote about the glorious Kingdom of God, he called it "the Kingdom of Heaven." Matthew is the only New Testament writer to use that phrase.

Matthew wrote urging his Christian readers to be prepared for that day and long sections of Jesus' teaching (notably Matthew 24–25) deal specifically with that subject. No matter what happens here, a judgment day is coming for all humankind. God's people must prepare for that day because they, more than anyone else, know it is coming and have every hope it will be a time of relief and blessing if they live according to the will of God. This is not "salvation by works." God's people are people of his kingdom. The only way to be a part of the rule of God (kingdom) in heaven is to be a part of the rule of God on the earth. That means God has to be seen as the ruling figure of one's life. That God is gracious to those who struggle to live this life, fail, and keep coming back to him is another fundamental point of Matthew's Gospel. It is why Matthew so often mentions Jesus' compassion for those who mourn the poverty of their own spirit and evidence total dependence on God.

Matthew is divided into nine sections, alternating between a "story" section and a "teaching" section. All the teaching sections begin with Jesus calling his disciples together. They all end the same way, with the words "when Jesus finished saying these things." An outline is as follows:

1) Story—Matthew 1–4
2) Teaching—Matthew 5–7
3) Story—Matthew 8–9
4) Teaching—Matthew 10
5) Story—Matthew 11–12
6) Teaching—Matthew 13
7) Story—Matthew 14–18
8) Teaching—Matthew 19–25
9) Story—Matthew 26–28

Matthew points us beyond this life to the life to come. He does not assure his readers they will receive that life, but reminds them of the requirements to receive it, the lifestyle necessary to receive it as a "reward," a word Matthew uses twelve times in his Gospel. Do not imagine Matthew is talking about salvation by works. He is writing to the saved. The reward is theirs to lose.

Mark

In the second century AD, Mark was remembered as a helper and close companion of Peter. He was a relative of Barnabas and a travel companion of both Barnabas and Paul on their first missionary journey (Acts 13–14). Early second-century writers, believing Mark not to be an eyewitness of Jesus' ministry, believed that Peter told Mark stories and Mark wrote them down; that became the Gospel of Mark. Some second-century Christians believed Mark wrote after Matthew, copying much of his work.

All of this presumed, of course, that the Gospel writers wrote simply to recount the life of Christ without any other motives. The evidence, however, is that all the Gospel writers shaped their narratives to make specific points to their intended readers. Thus, while they often include the same material, it is presented differently in order to make their God-inspired points.

Additionally, there is ample evidence that Mark, young as he was, did in fact witness at least some of the ministry of Jesus. His Gospel account is full of the kind of details that would be common only to an eyewitness. One Bible scholar has listed 200 details, mentioned only by Mark, in his first six chapters that would be the sort of thing only an eyewitness would know.

Mark grew up in a home of privilege in Jerusalem. He may have been the young man who fled without his clothes when Jesus' was arrested (Mark 14:51); but he is best known in the early history of the church because he abandoned Paul and Barnabas on their first missionary journey. This was his early reputation: when the going got tough, Mark "cut and ran." And yet his life became one of great faithfulness. He was with Paul in prison in Rome (Philemon 1:24) as well as with Peter (1 Peter 5:13). Near the end of his life, Paul sent for Mark to help him once again in Rome. Mark's personal story is one of spiritual growth—from a scared, faithless Christian to one of great faith.

As Mark presents his account of the gospel, he focuses less on what Jesus said and more on what Jesus did. He also focuses on the disciples, also known as "the twelve," and how they reacted to Jesus. More in Mark than in any other Gospel account, we hear Jesus' stinging rebukes toward his inner circle of followers for their lack of faith. Early Christians, reading Mark for the first time, would recognize that these bumbling, faithless men had become much different people, well known for their allegiance to Jesus. The readers would also be able to see themselves in the early lives of these men and take hope that they too could, like the twelve, become more mature if they would but stick with Jesus and follow his example. Such a transformation would be necessary if the early readers were to impact the world that so very much needed to hear the gospel.

Mark focuses on the Galilean part of Jesus' ministry, and everywhere Jesus goes in that region, he is well received. It is only when he goes to Jerusalem or meets people from Jerusalem that he encounters opposition. The very people who should have known, accepted, and welcomed Jesus, the people of Judaea, did not.

Mark is about discipleship, and Jesus' own disciples, the twelve, serve as an example of what discipleship is not. True disciples should see in their lives the behavior of Jesus, not the behavior of the disciples. Additionally, as people of faith, we must live out our faith, not with the comfort, restrictiveness, and closed-mindedness of the Jerusalem religious elite who rejected Jesus, but with the joy of a Galilean, a newcomer—an outcast who has been, by the grace of God, allowed into the inner circle.

Mark can be divided as follows:

I)   Introduction—Mark 1:1–15
II) Ministry Outside Jerusalem—Mark 1:16–10:31
III) Ministry and Death in Jerusalem—Mark
     10:32–16:20

Luke–Acts (Part 1)

The books of Luke and Acts of the Apostles together comprise the largest single body of literature in the New Testament.

In other words, while Paul penned more of the books than anyone else, the writer of Luke–Acts penned more of the New Testament than anyone else. Ancient scrolls ran about 30 to 35 feet in length. Both the Gospel of Luke and Acts are long enough to have taken one scroll each, and that is likely why Luke divided them into two books.

Luke was a medical doctor. He had been living in Troas when he teamed up with Paul on Paul's second missionary journey. From that point on, he was Paul's occasional traveling companion, accompanying him to Jerusalem at the end of his third mission trip and later to Rome. He was with Paul during both of his Roman imprisonments and these books were likely written near the end of the first one.

The books are addressed to a man named Theophilus who, because of the title Luke gave him ("most excellent"), may have been a high Roman official. Luke's stated purpose for writing (often overlooked in Bible classes) is that Theophilus might know the *certainty* of the things he had been taught. There are actually two issues here no one should miss when reading these books.

First, Luke and Acts were written to provide proof that the story of Christianity was true. Luke claims to have "carefully researched" his presentation. He provides names and often locations of important people who were involved in the story. Luke mentions the names of witnesses who would be favorable to the Christian story and the names of those who would not, but all are mentioned to verify the account. Though Luke himself was not an eyewitness to the ministry of Jesus, he repeatedly mentions the abundance of witnesses. He provides dates and gives locations for the events that occur. He mentions a number of trials for which there would be court records. All of this is presented so that his first reader could "check it out" and know that this is not fiction. The events really happened. Luke and Acts should be read with pencil and paper in hand, noting the evidence for the truthfulness of the Christian story. Until evidence, contemporary with either the events or Luke's account, arises to challenge the veracity of the story, Luke and Acts remain irrefutable evidence of the trustworthiness of the New Testament story.

Second, and equally important, Luke wrote that his first reader might know the certainty of *what he had been taught*. So what had Theophilus been taught? In reading Luke and Acts, we should be looking for the teaching Luke was seeking to verify. By discerning the recurring themes in these two books, we get an idea of what the early church focused on in its teaching. In the next section, I will review a few of those themes and provide an outline for the books.

Luke–Acts (Part 2)

As Luke opens part one of his two-part look at the story of Christianity, he gives his purpose for writing: "Since I myself have carefully investigated everything from the beginning, it seemed good also to me to write an orderly account for you, most excellent Theophilus, so that you may know the certainty of the things you have been taught" (Luke 1:3–4).

What was it Theophilus had been taught? At a time when Christianity was greatly opposed, what were Christians teaching about themselves and about Jesus? Repeated themes in Luke's books help us answer these questions. The following are but a few, but very important.

Christianity is the work of God. From Jesus' birth to the end of Acts, Luke notes that what has happened would simply be unexplainable were God not actively involved. Jesus is God. What he does, only God can do. What his followers do can only be accomplished if God is working through them.

Christianity is innocent. Written at a time when official Roman persecution of Christians was just beginning, Luke emphasizes that Christians are law-abiding citizens. Though often mistreated by public officials and hauled before kangaroo courts, Jesus and his followers are never convicted of any crimes—because they are not guilty. At the end of Luke Jesus is pronounced innocent three times—one of them by a Herodian king. At the end of Acts, Paul is likewise pronounced innocent of any crime three times. Again, one of those is a Herodian king.

Christianity is unstoppable. Reviewing the evidence, one should not imagine anyone would be able to stop or destroy Christianity. Lots of people tried. They all failed. They all failed because God is supreme, these are his people, and they are following his will. If the first reader was a Christian, the presence and power of God revealed in this story would be a tremendous incentive to faith. In the last section of Luke, Jesus determinedly goes to his death in Jerusalem. But Luke shows that none of this is happenstance. God is in control and what is happening is by his hand. The same is true in the last section of the book of Acts in the life of Paul.

Christianity is concerned with helping others, especially those who cannot help themselves. The poor, the ill, and the marginalized of society are the people Jesus is most attentive to, and that becomes a characteristic of God's people as the book of Acts unfolds. In a world where social standing played a huge role, Christians—men and women, rich and poor—stand alike in God's sight and live as equals.

The followers of Jesus are a people who take ethics seriously. Lying, stealing, immorality, and mistreating others is not tolerated among Christians, and the consequences of such behavior are often serious.

The followers of Jesus are a people who take unity seriously. Christians do not always behave as they should. But when they do not, their leadership takes special pains to address difficult matters and, as a group, unity prevails. They may not always agree, but they do make the effort to get along. The stories in Acts 7 and 15 detail the lengths to which the early church would go to maintain unity.

These are not the only themes, but they are repeated ones, ones we should pay attention to not only as we talk to others about Jesus and his people, but also as we try to live as Christians in the world.

Here is an outline of Luke and Acts:

I) Luke—Jesus: the Son of God
   A) God has come—1–4
   B) Proof: a section devoted to the miracles of Jesus –5–9
   C) Why Jesus' deity is important—because of what he taught.—9–19
   D) The will of God is unstoppable—20–24
II) Acts—Christians: The people of God
   A) In Jerusalem—1–7
   B) In Surrounding Areas—8–9
   C) Among the Gentiles—10–19
   D) The will of God is unstoppable—20–28

John

At the end of John we have these words: "Jesus did many other miraculous signs in the presence of his disciples, which are not recorded in this book. But these are written that you may believe that Jesus is the Christ, the Son of God, and that by believing you may have life in his name."

Most often, John's intent (writing that the reader might "believe") is mistakenly taken to mean that it was written to bring the unsaved to Christ. But John is a difficult book for one who doesn't already have an acquaintance with Christianity.

As the story opens, the reader is expected to know who John the Baptist is (without even calling him "the Baptist"). Jesus appears without warning or identification except for John the Baptist calling him "the Lamb of God who takes away the sin of the world." One has no idea where Jesus came from. The reader is expected to understand that the story takes place in Palestine, but is not expected to know Jewish customs or much about Palestinian geography. In other words, the reader of John is expected to already have some knowledge of the Jesus story—enough to have already become a Christian. (Note, for example, that John tells us that Mary, the sister of Lazarus, was the one who had poured perfume on the Lord and wiped his feet with her hair—11:2. John assumes his readers already know the story, because he doesn't tell it himself until the next chapter.)

But why then does John write to encourage "belief" among those who already believe? The answer lies in the meaning of the word "belief." Its basic meaning is to "trust," and that's something with which God's people have always struggled. It's one thing for me to mentally agree that Jesus is the Son of God. It is entirely another for me to trust Jesus. It requires little response from me to agree to Jesus' identity. But trusting Jesus requires action demonstrating that trust. John writes to convince his readers to do the latter.

The first 12 chapters of John proclaim the identity of Jesus. Jesus is called the "lamb of God," the "light and life of men," the "one on whom the Spirit of God resides," the "son of God" and the "king of Israel." Jesus himself claims God is his father, that he is the source of life, an equal to God who does God's work and speaks God's word. These are not just claims. In this section Jesus performs "signs" that demonstrate his power over matter, distance, time, resources, gravity, misfortune, and life itself. No one but God could do these things.

The next five chapters (13–17) contain Jesus' final words on the night he was betrayed; as you read them, you notice that John is using them to tell his readers how faith should be seen in their lives. Christians live their lives unafraid because they trust in God. Their goal is a home with God in heaven. They are obedient to God, and seek to remain in fellowship with Jesus. They are united with one another, and take life's challenges and needs to God in prayer, confident that he will answer their pleas. These are, John says, the marks of the trusting life, the marks of a believer.

The final chapters (18–21) concern Jesus death, burial, and resurrection, establishing the truthfulness of Jesus' claim to be able to take his life back from the dead (10:17–18). Peter's denial of Jesus also plays a prominent role in this section. The story ends not with Jesus' ascension, but with his forgiveness and acceptance of Peter. The picture of Jesus as one who can be trusted with one's life is complete. He doesn't give up on his people, but sticks with them, listening to them with the ear of God, and acting on their behalf with the power of God.

Romans

Probably no book of the New Testament has been more read and studied than Paul's letter to the Romans. Half a millennium ago, Martin Luther wrote: "This epistle is really the chief part of the New Testament, and is truly the purest gospel." His appreciation for this section of the Bible has been echoed by a host of Bible scholars since his day.

But for all the accolades heaped upon it, Romans was, and remains, simply a letter. Inspired by God to be sure and penned by the most famous of all the apostles and early Christianity's most successful missionary, it is a letter to a struggling local congregation in Rome. Its personal nature is underscored at the end where we find the longest list of Christians in any of the New Testament documents.

The letter was written in the middle of the first century. The church in Rome had been in existence for a number of years and had gone through many difficult times. It was composed of Jewish Christians and Gentile Christians, and therein lay the problem.

The Jewish Christians in the Roman church had a long history with God through their heritage, and they believed that gave them a better standing with God. That standing they called "righteousness." Righteousness was achieved because they were Jews, and being Jewish meant circumcision, observing dietary laws, and Jewish festivals. These were a means of securing righteousness, as well as evidence of their standing. Unfortunately, since those were the identifying marks, other areas of obedience, like trust in God, sexual purity, respect for authority, and looking after the needs of others, were short-changed.

The Gentile Christians, on the other hand, had no history with God. But they had been saved by grace through faith. If they could be saved without such a heritage, why did they need it? Their impulse was to get rid of everything Jewish. That, of course, included the Old Testament. Unfortunately, by getting rid of the Old Testament and focusing solely on salvation by grace, their lives ended up with little ethical direction.

In this letter, Paul walks a tightrope. On the one hand, he must insist that salvation has nothing to do with human actions (we can't save ourselves) and everything to do with the action of God. That won't make the Jewish Christians happy. On the other hand, he must insist that the Christian's standing with God, "righteousness," cannot be separated from obedience (and that won't make the Gentile Christians happy). And so, as he begins, he speaks of the good news of God, that through Jesus Christ people have been called to an obedience which proceeds from faith.

The first section of Romans is chapters 1–8. Here Paul insists that one's standing with God cannot be achieved by behavior. If it could, they would have no standing because they are living sinful lives (1–3). Standing with God has been secured by Jesus' sacrifice and the trust we place in what *he* did rather than what *we* do (3–5). And yet, our standing with God cannot be divorced from behavior, for in Christ we have been called to a new way of living, empowered by God himself (6–8).

In the second section (9–11), Paul says the Jewishness of the gospel cannot be dismissed, nor should it be. But neither should Jewishness be thought of as the basis of one's standing with God. These Christians, divided along racial, ethnic, and traditional lines, must learn to get along and appreciate one another.

The third section (12–16) deals with how the faith that saves is evidenced in life—what real standing with God (righteousness) looks like. Interestingly, the largest part of this section is devoted to Christians getting along with each other.

The Christian church still suffers from division. No matter what the cause or who is right or wrong, the existence of division demonstrates a misunderstanding of faith and a lack of appreciation for the work of God and the high calling that is ours.

1 Corinthians

The books of 1 and 2 Corinthians comprise over half of Paul's writing in the New Testament. It is the largest body of Paul's writings.

Paul wrote 1 Corinthians on his third missionary journey (Acts 19:1–21:16) while still in Ephesus (1 Corinthians 16:8). It was written to the Christians who comprised the church in Corinth, a major city in Greece. The metropolis was decidedly Roman in its customs and decidedly worldly in everything. It was impressive in its architecture and, as one of three banking centers in Greece, exceedingly rich. One writer puts it like this: "The only Corinthian tradition . . . respected was commercial success. It was every man for himself and the weak went to the wall" [Jerome Murphy-O'Connor, *The Theology of the Second Letter to the Corinthians* (Cambridge: Cambridge University Press, 1991), 5]. Additionally, like all major cities, it was a city filled with vice.

Honor and respect were hugely important. Ben Witherington writes: "The Corinthian people lived within an honor-shame cultural orientation, where public recognition was often more important than facts and where the worst thing that could happen was for one's reputation to be publicly tarnished. In such a culture a person's sense of worth is based on recognition of one's accomplishments" [Ben Witherington III, *Conflict and Community in Corinth* (Grand Rapids, MI: Eerdmans, 1995), 8]. Interestingly, of the 1,553 monuments recovered from the ancient world, 1,200 of them are from Corinth [Anthony Thistleton, *The First Epistle to the Corinthians* (Grand Rapids, MI: Eerdmans, 2000), 5].

The church was deeply divided along lines of worldly status. Some believed they could get away with anything, even if they were Christians, because of their status. Others, of lower status, made it their aim to "get back" at the upper crust. At heart, the problem was simply worldliness.

The book may be outlined as follows:

1) The importance of unity, and the status that comes from God (1–4)
2) Dealing with sin in interpersonal relationships (5–6)
3) Matters dealing with marriage (7)
4) Getting along with fellow Christians (8–10)
5) Disorder in the worship assembly (11–14)
6) The resurrection (15)
7) Plans for the future (16)

More is written about the resurrection in 1 Corinthians than anywhere else in the New Testament. The discussion at first seems oddly out of place in a book devoted to resolving the problems of disunity, but its position at the end of the book is pointedly relevant. To a group of people bent on "living for today," Paul reminds them that there is a greater day coming, and they should live in view of that day. In the middle of discussing the resurrection, he writes: "Do not be misled: 'Bad company corrupts good character.' Come back to your senses as you ought, and stop sinning; for there are some who are ignorant of God—I say this to your shame" (1 Corinthians 15:33–34). In the same chapter, to these Christians whose self-worth was bound up in their worldly status and accomplishments, Paul wrote: "I declare to you, brothers, that flesh and blood cannot inherit the kingdom of God, nor does the perishable inherit the imperishable" (15:50).

We live in a world very much like Corinth, and that world influences us as much as it did them. The message of this book is as much for us as it was for them. As Christians, we must leave the "wisdom of the world" (considered "foolishness" by God) behind, and come together in the body of Christ, dedicated to one another with the same dedication we give Jesus, living by a heavenly standard, for we are Christ's body on the earth.

2 Corinthians

Paul's letters to the church in Corinth comprise the largest body of Paul's writings. In fact, Paul wrote them more letters than we actually have—at least two more that we know of. What we call 2 Corinthians is the most personal of all Paul's letters.

Paul wrote this letter while on his third mission trip. The Christians in Judea at this time were struggling economically. There had been a famine. Also, by accepting Christ they had been cut off from family and friends, and likely even had their businesses shunned. Paul believed that Christians from other churches should help. There was a spiritual dimension to this plea as well: If Gentile churches would help Jewish churches, that would further reinforce the intent of Jesus that all God's people regard themselves as one—free from ethnic, social, and political barriers.

At the end of 1 Corinthians, Paul asked the Christians there to take up collections for this cause. They weren't the only ones he asked. He also petitioned churches in Asia Minor, as well as other churches throughout Greece.

Everywhere Paul asked, the response was overwhelming—everywhere except Corinth. At first, they responded favorably. But then, they lagged in getting it done. The Corinthian Christians objected to Paul telling them what to do. He did not, after all, fit their notion of a successful person. He was not the sort of polished speaker they were accustomed to. And what gave him the right to speak so boldly to them about how they should be living and conducting their worship assemblies? He wasn't even one of "the twelve" disciples of Jesus!

Paul had written to them intending to meet his co-worker Titus in Troas and then come straight to Corinth. But Titus didn't show. Worried about him, Paul changed his travel plans to go look for Titus in Macedonia. The Corinthians, not knowing the whole story, mistakenly construed this to mean Paul wasn't very organized and couldn't follow through on his plans, further alienating him from them.

Second Corinthians can be divided into parts as follows:

I)   Paul's reminder to them of what it means to live the Christian life (1–7)
II) Paul's explanation of the collection for the poor in Judea (8–9)
III) Paul's defense of his ministry (10–13)

This letter is a reminder to Christians in all times that our perspective should be different from the world's. Ours is not a "surface" perspective, and our standards are not those of the world (2 Corinthians 10:2, 7). We should purge our lives of everything that keeps us from seeing with the perspective of God.

How did the Corinthians respond? Not well, in my opinion. When Paul finally delivers the collection to Jerusalem, there are representatives from every contributing church . . . with the exception of Corinth.

Galatians

In all probability, the book of Galatians is the earliest letter we have from Paul. It was written on his second missionary journey, probably from Corinth, and would have addressed Christians in the cities of Antioch, Iconium, Lystra, and Derbe.

Christianity grew out of Judaism. God planned it that way, but because of it, many of the problems of Judaism also plagued early Christianity. There was a tendency to believe that in order to be a Christian one had to first become a Jew; after all, the earliest Christians were Jews and the Christians used the Jewish scriptures. Judaism had, by that time, focused narrowly on three areas: observing the sabbath, circumcision, and observing dietary laws. These observances also became a part of life in the early church (including, for Judean Christians, observing the traditional hours of prayer).

There was nothing inherently wrong with observing these things. The problem lay with an attendant belief—that doing these things made a person "right" with God and qualified one to receive God's favor.

This belief that one could, by one's own actions, put God in one's debt is the technical description for what today we call "legalism," and it was precisely the difficulty facing the Galatian churches. Some Christians were relying (2:10) on circumcision and the observance of religious holidays (4:10). Furthermore, these Christians were eager to win other Christians to their way of thinking (4:17) in order to avoid being ostracized by non-Christian Jews (6:12). The controversy threw the Christian church there into confusion (5:10) by compelling the other Christians to conform to this teaching (6:12).

Paul calls this (reliance on circumcision, observance of festival days and dietary laws) "observing" the law. It is important to keep this in mind. "Observing the law," to Paul, was not "being obedient to the Old Testament." It was, in context, keeping the rules in *these three areas* so as to earn God's favor.

This teaching removed trust in Christ's sacrifice and God's grace from the Christian picture. It resulted in people who, having fulfilled the requirements in these three areas, felt perfectly free to live as they pleased in other areas of life. Paul said this teaching was so insidious that those who held it had fallen from grace (5:4) and those who taught it deserved eternal condemnation (1:8–9). In its rebuke of Christians, Galatians is Paul's harshest letter.

The following is an outline of the letter:

I) Paul pointedly attacks the issue and establishes his authority to address it. 1:1–2:21
II) The false teaching they are accepting is contrary to the Galatians' experience, contrary to the example of Abraham, contrary to scripture itself, and contrary to the promise of God. 3:1–29
III) The false teaching they are accepting is making them less than what God has in mind for them. 4:1–5:15

IV) The life of faith calls them not to outward ritual,
   but to a lifestyle that demonstrates that God dwells
   in each of them. 5:16–6:18

When we are tempted to think we, or others, deserve the grace of God because of what we have done or how we have lived, Galatians stands as Christ's call to place our confidence not in ourselves, but in what God has done through Christ. It also reminds us that what we believe influences what we do, and therefore is just as important. When what we believe is not according to Scripture or a misunderstanding of Scripture, it can lead us to behavior that is not only inadequate but spiritually fatal.

Ephesians

In the ancient world Ephesus was the largest trading city in Asia Minor (now Turkey)—and by far the richest. It was also a world center for religious activity. While there on his third missionary journey, Paul also made it a center for Christian evangelism. He spent three years there. The church grew and its members were well versed in the faith. The future of God's people in Ephesus should have been bright.

But dark clouds loomed on the horizon. The same challenges we face in a high profile metropolitan community faced them. Paul believed that after he left the congregation's strategic position and leadership would make it a ripe target for Satan. At the end of his third missionary journey, he warned the Ephesian leadership of this possibility (Acts 20:17–31). But either the warning was unheeded or it wasn't enough. Four years later the church was in trouble, wrecked by conflict, greed, immorality, and dysfunctional families.

There were three reasons for Satan's success there:

First, the Christians forgot what God had done for them and who he had called them to be. Second, they were no longer living like children of God, grateful for their redemption from sin and place in God's family. The world could no longer see God in them. Third, faced with the reality of their plight, they attempted to change without God's help—and they failed. These three problems help us to see a three-part outline of Ephesians.

I)   Paul tells them they are special to God, and reminds them of why they are special and how they got that way (1–3).

II) He tells them what being special to God is supposed to look like in their lives (4:1–6:9).

III) He tells them how this can be accomplished through the power, not of themselves, but of God (6:10–23).

The Ephesians had every reason to get the message. But thirty years later, God told them: "You've left your first love" (Revelation 2:4). Their failure should not be lost on us.

Philippians

The city of Philippi was a predominately Gentile community in the northern part of Greece. The Romans made it a colony, meaning that they retired soldiers from their legions there. Paul established a church in Philippi during his second missionary journey. This congregation became very dear to him. Normally, Paul did not take financial support from churches he served, but Philippi was different. So dear was he to them that they sent aid to him several times (Philippians 4:15–16). So attached were they to his work that, even though the church in Philippi was very poor, they still joined in the collection Paul took for the suffering Christians in Judea (2 Corinthians 8:2).

It was during his first imprisonment in Rome that Paul wrote his letter to the Philippians. At the time, two women of that church, well known for their good works and faithfulness, had a disagreement. The congregation began to take sides and division occurred. It did not help that the Philippian church was also undergoing persecution. This scenario became the impetus for Paul's letter to them. In his opening, Paul urges the church to "stand firm in one spirit, contending as one man for the faith of the gospel" (1:27).

Division occurs when people forget that God has called us to humility and putting the welfare of others above ourselves. In the first three chapters of Philippians, Paul cites four examples of personal sacrifice for the good of others. He cites himself (1 and 3), Christ, Timothy, and Epaphroditus (2). His point is that Christians, in following Christ's example and that of followers the Philippians knew, should "do nothing out of selfish ambition or vain conceit, but in humility consider others first" (2:3–4).

In chapter four, based on the examples he has cited, Paul focuses on the Philippians' problem specifically and urges a resolution of the conflict among themselves, and a trust in God to take care of the persecution.

Colossians & Philemon

Located in what today is south central Turkey, the city of Colossae was once great and prosperous. But times change. By the days of the apostle Paul, Colossae was a broken metropolis living on past glory. The main highway no longer passed through its precincts, and travelers hurried on by to Laodicea a few miles to the north and west.

Christianity was brought to Colossae by Epaphras who had come into contact, if not with Paul, then at least with Christianity, in his travels. Though there is no evidence that Paul ever visited this church, he knew a number of its members: Epaphras, Archippus, Philemon, Apphia, and Nymphas.

While imprisoned in Rome in the early 60s AD, Paul met a runaway slave named Onesimus. Paul shared the gospel with him and Onesimus became a Christian.

Christianity does not approve of slavery. In fact, the buying and selling of slaves is forbidden (1 Timothy 1:10). But Christianity came into a world where slavery was a norm. Many slaves and slave owners became Christians. Christian slave owners were themselves slaves of God. A master's treatment of his slave was supposed to mirror the benevolence of God toward the master. Christian slaves were to offer their masters the same submission the slaves offered Jesus.

Onesimus, of course, having become a Christian, would have to return to his master. Imagine Paul's surprise when he learned that Onesimus' former master was Paul's old friend, Philemon of Colossae.

About this same time, Paul learned that the church in Colossae was having a difficult time. False teachers were teaching that Christianity was a system of asceticism involving strict dietary laws and ritualism involving the observance of special festival days. Perhaps that would not be too bad, but the false teachers went on to emphasize that Christians *made themselves* acceptable to God by observing these things. And if that weren't enough, they added the worship of angels to their list of spiritual practices.

This teaching created two problems. First, it took the focus of the Christian faith off what God had done through Christ, and placed it on what the Colossian Christians were doing. Second, by emphasizing the importance of religious ritual, they took the emphasis off the more important requirements of living the Christian life (moral purity, compassion, honesty, tolerance, submission) in favor of dietary laws and observances.

Paul wrote the letter to the Colossians to deal with these problems. He sent it by the hand of his co-worker, Tychicus, who accompanied Onesimus back to his hometown and master, Philemon. The letter to Philemon reminded the master how he was supposed to treat his slaves as Onesimus returned to him, now no longer a slave but a brother in Christ.

Colossians can be divided into two sections:

I) The focus for who we are and what we believe is not us but Jesus and what he has done for us. 1–2
II) Because of what Jesus has done and who we have become, our behavior should be characterized by the lifestyle described in these chapters. 3–4.

Thessalonians

The book of Acts recounts three separate mission trips taken by Paul. The first journey (Acts 13–14) focused on establishing Christian congregations on Cyprus and in south central and southeastern Asia Minor. The second journey (Acts 16–18) recounts the beginning of the church in Greece with Paul in the lead. The third journey (Acts 19–21) details Paul's work in establishing the church throughout Asia Minor from the city of Ephesus, and ends with him traveling to Jerusalem.

The second journey was filled with difficulties. Early on, hindrances in Asia Minor dogged their every move. Finally, Paul and his companions crossed the Aegean Sea and went to Philippi. A church was started there, but not without considerable persecution. The group moved to Thessalonica, the capital city of Macedonia, but again found themselves opposed by both Jewish and Gentile authorities. The opposition was so extreme that some of the new converts were forced to post a bond, obligating them to financial penalties if unrest arose again in the city. The Christians had no intention of causing trouble, but they could not speak for their opponents who would stop at nothing to persecute the young movement then taking the world by storm. To avoid trouble for the young church in Thessalonica, Paul and his coworker Silas left town under cover of night for the quieter refuge of a town off the beaten track to the south, Berea.

In Acts, Luke is careful to note that all the persecutions came from people who, for a variety of selfish reasons, opposed the gospel of Christ. But surely it *looked* to the public as if Paul and his companions were just a group of troublemakers, and the new Christians left behind in those cities would suffer tremendous ridicule. Additionally, would not the new converts wonder why, if these men were truly emissaries of God, they had to endure so much opposition?

Paul knew how it looked. And so, not so very long after leaving Thessalonica, he wrote the first and then second letter to the Thessalonians. In the first letter, he reminds them that, unlike so many traveling philosophers of his day, Paul, rather than take support from his converts, instead supported them, caring for them as a mother or a father would care for their child (1 and 2).

In chapter three he compliments them on their behavior since he left, and in chapters four and five gives this young church direction for living the Christian life.

But the Thessalonian church was vulnerable from the outside. The pagan world found the thought of a resurrected Jesus too much of a stretch. The idea that he would come back and take his people home to heaven was even more ludicrous. To harass the Christians further, someone wrote a letter to the church in Thessalonica telling them Jesus had come already—and they had missed it. The authors signed Paul's name to the document.

The Thessalonian church was vulnerable from the inside as well. They were new to Christianity and Paul did not have enough time to teach them fully. Some thought Jesus was coming back right away. They quit their jobs, "waiting" on the Lord. Those who were still working felt an obligation to support those who weren't. Hadn't Paul's example been to care for those in need?

Second Thessalonians was written specifically to address these two issues. He told them obviously Jesus had not come yet because they were still being persecuted and tempted. Had Jesus already come, their opponents, including the devil, would have already been destroyed (1–2). In the final chapter, he reminded them that, until Jesus came, they should *all* work. And if some Christians would not, they should be removed from the fellowship of believers.

It is important to remember that this was a young church. Aside from the obvious doctrinal and ethical instruction the books offer, they also help us understand what Paul believed was most important for new Christians to know.

Letters to Timothy

The book of Acts ends with mention of Paul's two-year house arrest in Rome. From what we can tell from Paul's letters to Timothy and Titus, he was released from prison after that time and allowed to travel once again. He returned to Ephesus where he preached for a while before going on to Greece and then to Crete. He spent at least a winter at the Greek resort town of Nicopolis, and returned to Asia Minor before being arrested once again and sent back to Rome. At some point during these travels, Paul left Timothy in Ephesus to help that church (1 Timothy 1:3).

Timothy was no newcomer to helping churches through difficult times. It had been his ministry virtually from the beginning. When we are first introduced to him (48 AD; Acts 16), Timothy is already highly respected by churches in the cities of Derbe and Lystra. Not long after meeting Paul, one of his first assignments was to help the fledgling Thessalonian congregation. On Paul's next journey, Timothy was sent to deal with the division in Corinth. Paul had asked Apollos to go, but Apollos had refused (1 Corinthians 4:17; 16:12). Just after Paul's imprisonment in Rome, he sent Timothy to deal with the division of the Philippian church. Paul wrote: "I have no one else like him, who takes a genuine interest in your welfare. For everyone looks out for his own interests, not those of Jesus Christ. But you know that Timothy has proved himself . . ." (Philippians 2:20–22).

First and Second Timothy are letters written twenty years after Paul met Timothy. There was a power struggle in the Ephesian church, and Paul left Timothy in Ephesus to deal with the issues and to cultivate purity of heart, a sincere faith, and a clean conscience among the members.

Perhaps it was a mid-life crisis or just discouragement at the enormity of his task, but for whatever reason, Timothy became a part of the problem rather than the solution. He took sides in the quarrels and by the time of the first letter, he'd begun thinking in some fairly materialistic terms. Note the following instructions to him in the first letter:

> Timothy, my son, I give you this instruction in keeping with the prophecies once made about you, so that by following them you may fight the good fight, holding on to faith and a good conscience. Some have rejected these and so have shipwrecked their faith. . . . I write these things to you hoping to come to you quickly, but if I am delayed, that you will know how to behave in the house of God . . . . Stop neglecting your gift . . . . Be diligent in these matters; give yourself wholly to them, so that everyone may see your progress. Watch your life and doctrine closely. Persevere in them . . . . Stop listening to accusations against Elders . . . keep these instructions without partiality, and to do nothing out of favoritism . . . do not share in the sins of others. Keep yourself pure. . . . flee [the desire to get rich] and pursue righteousness, godliness, faith, love, endurance and gentleness. . . . Turn away from godless chatter . . ." (1:18–19; 3:15; 4:14–15; 5:19, 21–22; 6:11, 20).

We are not sure where Timothy is by the second letter, but we know he was having a difficult time. His zeal was about to die. Paul urges him not to be ashamed of him, nor of Jesus (1:8), but to "be strong" and to avoid becoming involved in worldly affairs (2:1–4). At the end of the letter, Paul urges him to come see him soon—even though Paul is in a Roman prison for the second time. Paul knows the only release he will get this time will be in death.

Did Timothy make it to Rome in time? Did he renew his zeal?

I believe he did. The writer of Hebrews mentions that Timothy has been "released" and that, if he arrives in time, he and Timothy will come see the readers together (Hebrews 13:23).

We are all servants of God, and our ministries don't always go smoothly. Paul's letters to Timothy provide direction for the church, but mainly for those who serve, reminding them of what is important when the world gets us off course.

Letter to Titus

We don't know a lot about Titus. His name occurs only thirteen times in the New Testament, mostly in 2 Corinthians. He was a Gentile and probably an early leader in the church at Antioch.

In 48 AD, at the end of Paul's first missionary journey, some Jerusalem Christians went to Antioch and taught that one couldn't be a Christian unless one first, or also, became a Jew. The Antioch congregation, predominately Gentile, was visibly upset. The teaching appeared to have the sanction of the church in Jerusalem. A delegation was sent to Jerusalem to see if, in fact, this doctrine was being taught there. Titus was one of those delegates.

In Jerusalem, though some Christians did hold this errone-ous teaching, the church as a whole sent word that it was cer-tainly not the position of the church there nor its leadership. Paul mentions this event in Galatians and writes in a compli-mentary way of Titus' strength of character.

Despite this trouble and their ethnic differences, the Gentile Christians in Antioch had a warm affection for their Jewish brothers and sisters in Jerusalem. During a time of famine, even though the Antioch church was also affected, they took up a collection for the poor Christians in Jerusalem. As time went on, other Gentile Christians, realizing their deep indebtedness to the mission efforts of the Jerusalem church, also began to contribute to the church there. Titus, from Antioch, was one of those involved in organizing this relief effort and he was particularly involved in securing contributions from the church in Corinth.

Later, after Paul's first Roman imprisonment, Titus accompanied him on a mission to the island of Crete. If ever there was a place that needed the gospel, it was Crete. The men were known worldwide as thugs and layabouts. The children were known as "ill-bred" and greed and alcoholism were openly acceptable. One ancient writer described them this way: "It would be impossible to find, except in some rare instances, personal conduct more treacherous or public policy more unjust than in Crete" (Polybius, *Histories*, 6.47.5).

Churches were established on the island, and Paul, moving on to Italy, left Titus to develop leaders among the new Christians. Titus, however, became embroiled in a number of petty controversies which distracted him from his mission. Paul's letter to Titus served as a stinging reminder of his true task and gave him direction for accomplishing it. Often overlooked by Bible students are Paul's opening words: "The reason I left you in Crete was that you might straighten out what was left unfinished and appoint elders in every town, *as I directed you.*" The obvious implication is that Titus was failing in his mission.

The work of the church is not complicated. It is: living as Jesus lived, bringing others to Jesus, and encouraging others to follow your example. Leaders in this enterprise must be aware of how necessary and far-reaching are their examples, and train up others to take their place. We all live with the reality that one day our work here, like Titus' work on Crete, will come to an end. The only thing that will matter is how well we have adhered to this very simple mission. The book of Titus is a call to us all to remember the work God has given us to do, and not get side-tracked.

Hebrews

Nearly a half century ago, British Bible scholar F. F. Bruce wrote the following: "Of all the precious writings that speak of the Christian faith, it is doubtful if any makes a more distinctive contribution than the Epistle to the Hebrews. It describes in an elevated, incomparable way the true nature and value of the Christian religion. For the author of the Epistle, Christianity is the better and best of all possible religions. Beside it, there is no other" [F.F. Bruce, *The Epistle to the Hebrews* (Grand Rapids, MI: Eerdmans, 1964), xii].

Hebrews is, first and foremost, a letter. The writer knows his audience, knows their circumstances, and hopes to see them soon. Both the writer and the readers know Timothy, the apostle Paul's fellow worker in preaching the gospel. Both the writer and the readers are at home with the Greek translation of the Old Testament—for the writer quotes from it extensively and exclusively.

The first readers had gone through some difficult times because of their faith. The writer says they had been publicly exposed to insult and persecution, and had had their property confiscated (Hebrews 10:33–34). Tough times and lots of temptation had led the first readers of Hebrews to lose confidence in their faith, become less interested in one another, more concerned with self, and more susceptible to sin.

Surely, they thought, there had to be an easier religion!

I've got one for them! What about a religion that's mostly ritual? You know the sort: one where you can pray, go through some religious motions, pretty much do your own thing, and yet still be considered "faithful." A religion where there's a heavy emphasis on self-satisfaction, not a lot of accountability, and certainly not a lot of obligation. It would also need a mixture of "tradition" to give it respectability.

It was this kind of religion, heavily dosed with Old Testament roots, that was being embraced by the first recipients of Hebrews.

The book of Hebrews presents two realities: The first is in heaven; the second is on the earth. The earth is but a shadow or reflection of heaven. "Religion," as presented in the Old Testament, was but a shadow of what God intended. God, according to the writer of Hebrews, bridged the distance between those two realities in Jesus, his son. Jesus, though he was God, came to earth and lived as a human, where he experienced first-hand what we all experience—yet without sinning. He offered himself as a sacrifice for our sins and made possible an agreement between us and God. He became our eternal High Priest and opened the way for us to confidently come before God and find help in difficult times. What Jesus provides is better than tradition and better than ritual. In Jesus, we have a secure promise of rest with God—rest from all that tears our current lives apart. This is the message of the first ten chapters of the book.

In chapter eleven, the writer lists an honor roll of people who were traditionally held in high esteem because of their trust in God. The writer says they didn't have the same access to God Christians have, but they hung on to God in trying times anyway. That's what made these heroes memorable and venerable. If *they* could hold on, why couldn't the readers of this book?

Throughout Hebrews, the writer warns of the dangers of not holding on, of listening to themselves rather than to God, and of trusting in ritual and what seems religious rather actually trusting in God and living a holy life. The consequences, according to Hebrews, are eternal. As much as any New Testament book, perhaps more than most, the inspired writer underscores the important and inseparable connection between faith in and obedience to God. *What* that obedience entails, for the first readers of Hebrews, is specifically spelled out in the final two chapters.

God has spoken. One would be foolish to ignore him.

Making religion more palatable to our own tastes is not new. Neither is God's distaste for the result. Our age and temptations are not new. God has not changed. The message of Hebrews remains relevant for our time.

James

As far as we know, Mary and Joseph had at least four other boys after Jesus: James, Joseph, Simon, and Jude (Matthew 13:55). There were also some sisters whose names we don't know. During Jesus' life, his ministry was, at times, an embarrassment to his family. On one occasion, they thought he had lost his mind. Like most parents, however, no matter what they think of their children's actions, they stand with them to the bitter end. Mary, we know, was at the cross and likely was one of the women who tended Jesus' body the following Sunday.

When Jesus rose from the dead, he made a special appearance to his family, and that seems to have been a turning point in their perceptions. Within a few years James would become a pillar of the church in Jerusalem and both he and Jude would write two books included in the New Testament.

The first readers of James faced many of the same challenges Christians today face. There is the challenge of outright opposition from the world. There is the continual challenge of being lured by the world into thinking and acting like the world. There is the challenge presented simply by the difficulty of living a holy life. James calls Christians to realize that our faith requires decisive commitment. Note these directives:

- Don't merely *listen* to the word [of God]. *Do* what it says. 1:22
- What good is it to *say* you have faith if faith is not seen in your actions? *That* faith cannot save. (2:14).
- Who is wise and understanding among you? Let him show it by his good life, by deeds done in the humility that comes from wisdom. 3:13
- Wash your hands, you sinners, and purify your hearts, you double-minded. 4:8
- Don't grumble against each other, brothers, or you will be judged. The Judge is standing at the door! 5:9

I suggest that James 4:4 is a good theme verse for this book: "You adulterous people, don't you know that friendship with the world is hatred toward God? Anyone who chooses to be a friend of the world becomes an enemy of God." Keep in mind that James wrote to Christians. People who want to be at ease with the world and at ease with God have charted for themselves an impossible course that can only end in failure.

Half-hearted prayer, blaming God for your troubles (and your lack of successes), a loose tongue, discrimination against and mistreatment of the poor, an unwillingness to help the needy, planning without regard for God's will in your daily activities, and giving up when the going gets tough. These traits are all covered by James, and he writes of them in an unmistakable, condemnatory way.

For far too long Christians have suffered at the hands of those who hate us because we don't practice what we preach. Christianity is more, much, much more, than the positions we hold on hot-button issues (which, however, is all too often all the world knows of us). Christianity is a way of life built on a foundation of authentic faith. That's what James was calling his first readers to. And that is its message for us today.

Peter's Letters

Any presentation of a New Testament document that does not address practical behavior misses by a wide margin the intent of the book. This point is easily seen in the shorter books like James and Peter's letters.

Peter is the best known of the twelve apostles and the most often mentioned in the New Testament. But while much is written *about* him, we have only a little written *by* him—just two letters comprising a total of eight chapters. Both letters were written near the end of his life. Tradition holds that Peter was crucified upside down in Rome about 68 AD.

First Peter was written to Christians in Asia Minor who were undergoing great persecution. If you look up "suffer" in all its forms in a concordance, you will find it mentioned more in 1 Peter than in any other book of the Bible. Peter reminds his fellow Christians that Christ also suffered at the hands of unjust men and therefore they are simply following in Jesus' footsteps. Peter reminds his readers who they are:

- God's elect, chosen according to God's eternal plan to be obedient to him.
- Called to be holy, because God is holy.
- Royalty and priests entrusted with the task of declaring the praises of God.

Considering their high calling, Peter reminds his readers they should act accordingly, and tells them precisely what is expected of them. Peter does not tell his readers that their troubles will soon be over or that God will deliver them in this life. Instead, he reminds them that deliverance will be found in the life to come.

Second Peter focuses on two of Christianity's basic challenges: is the gospel message reliable and is it unchangeable? Peter provides evidence for its trustworthiness, and warns against trying to change it to make it more palatable to worldly tastes. But he doesn't stop there. A trustworthy message is valueless if it makes no impact on the lives of the hearers. One cannot do what one doesn't know to do. But knowing and not being obedient is the same as ignorance—and God will judge both. There is no excuse for a Christian not knowing the will of God. And even less for not being obedient.

1 John

All New Testament books address the matter of proper behavior. In the case of the letters, it is usually poor behavior that is addressed, along with the imperative to change. Thus in Romans Paul writes: "How shall we who died to sin live any longer in it?" (6:1). In Ephesians it is: "you should no longer walk as the rest of the Gentiles walk, in the futility of their mind" (4:17). In Colossians Paul writes: "Since you died with Christ to the basic principles of this world, why, as though you still belonged to it, do you submit to its rules?" (Colossians 2:20)

In 1 John, a call to change in behavior among Christians is precisely in mind. John, the disciple most close to Jesus, wrote this letter in the later years of his life to Christians:

- who claim to have fellowship with Christ yet walk "in darkness" (1:6).
- who (amazingly) claim to be without sin (1:8).
- who claim an intimacy with God and Jesus but who do not live according to their direction (2:3–4).
- who are in love with the world and its ways, but claim to love as God loves (2:15).
- who claim to love God, but do nothing to help the needy (3:17–18).

John writes that such behavior is an intolerable contradiction, and those who live it and advocate it are hypocrites and liars—fairly tough language.

Among those addressed in this letter were Christians who advocated this kind of life. The logical conclusion of their religious philosophy (if not their specific claim) was that Jesus—who he was and what he taught—didn't really matter. John calls them (and there is more than one, he says) "antichrists." The word only occurs in the first two letters of John. Whoever they were, they were a part of the Christian fellowship being addressed. That brings me to the following:

First, popular religious authors commonly describe "the antichrist" as some world leader, a messenger empowered by Satan, who will arise to lead the world against Christians and deceive Christians into leaving the fold. Customarily, the "antichrist" is paired with the "man of lawlessness" of 2 Thessalonians. But in describing the antichrist, authors and teachers would do well to confine themselves to the texts where the specific identification is made. An antichrist is *anyone* who undermines our submission to the authority of Jesus. It can be a non-Christian, but it is likely also to be a Christian.

Second, this attempt to identify the "antichrist" as some well-placed political figure, and the attempt to see him in our own history, leads Christians away from focusing on their own behavior and submitting to the will of Jesus. In doing that, one easily misses the primary message of 1 John: that how we behave determines whether Christians are *really* disciples or just hypocrites.

Third, John ties belief to behavior. "Whoever believes that Jesus is the Christ is born of God," he writes (5:1). We get sidetracked here into the discussion of whether *belief* is enough to be a Christian. John doesn't write simply that the one who believes is "born of God," but rather that the one who believes and is born of God *loves* others who are likewise born of God and keep God's commands (1 John 4:19–5:2). John is not discussing *how* one becomes a Christian or how one is saved, but how the saved person *acts* toward other saved people. After all, John is not writing to the unsaved but to Christians.

Finally, this point about Christian behavior is specifically underscored at least three times in the letter. First, in 2:6, "the person who claims to live in Jesus must live like Jesus lived." Second, in 3:2–3, "we are children of God; and it has not yet been revealed what we shall be, but we know that when Jesus is revealed, we shall be like Him, for we shall see Him as He is. And everyone who has this hope in Him keeps on purifying himself, just as Jesus is pure." Third, in 3:9, "No one who is born of God will continue to sin, because God's seed remains in him; he cannot go on sinning, because he has been born of God." In this text, it isn't that a Christian *cannot* sin, but that he or she simply no longer has that option.

Hypocrisy by Christians will not be overlooked by the world. First John is a bold declaration that it is not overlooked by God either.

2 John

John, one of Jesus' closest disciples, wrote four documents in the New Testament: the Gospel bearing his name and three letters. The first letter was written to a congregation of Christians. The second was written to a Christian woman whose name we do not know, and the third to a Christian man whose name was Gaius.

Women played an important role in the story of the New Testament. Devout women enabled Jesus and his disciples to preach in Galilee by supplying support for them (Luke 8:2–3). When Jesus left Galilee the final time for Judea, the twelve apostles understood he was heading into a political hornets' nest that might possibly take his life (John 11:16). They went with him anyway, as did some of the women who had been supporting the ministry. When Jesus was led to be crucified, women were mourning and crying for him along the way. Matthew tells us there were *many* women who watched the crucifixion from a distance. Women were the last to leave the cross. They were the first to arrive at Jesus' tomb on Sunday.

As the gospel spread, women continued to play important roles. When Saul's persecution laid waste the church in Jerusalem, Christian men and women were seen as equal threats to the social order and the persecution made no distinction between them (Acts 8:3; 9:2). When the gospel reached Greece, women were the first converts and the house of Lydia became headquarters for Paul and his companions for their mission work in Philippi. As he ended his letter to the Romans, Paul recommended Phoebe, a Christian from Cenchrea (in Greece) who had come to Rome (perhaps delivering Paul's letter). He mentions Priscilla, who played a pivotal role in converting Apollos, a great preacher of the gospel. He also mentions a Mary who played an important role in the Roman church, along with Herodian, Tryphena, Tryphosa, Persis, and Junia, who had been imprisoned for her faith.

John does not supply us with the name of the woman addressed in 2 John, but she, like the mother of Timothy, had been a wholesome influence on her children and they had deserved reputations of their own in the Christian community.

Though not their only work, women provided crucial hospitality to missionaries traveling in the ancient world. Unfortunately, not every missionary had the purest of motives. There were those who proclaimed that Jesus was not really human. Some took the view that he only seemed to be human, because surely God would not really become a man. This was a conflation of both Christianity and paganism.

It did make a difference. If Jesus was not a man, then he could not have borne our sins on the cross. If he were not a man, he did not provide an example of holy living for humankind to follow. In essence, if he were not human, then he lied. The doctrine undermined the very foundation of the Christian faith.

But what if a Christian missionary came preaching this doctrine? How should his brothers and sisters in Christ regard him? When it was a hallmark of Christianity to show hospitality to everyone, how should they treat the false teacher?

Writing to this wonderful Christian woman, John emphasized the importance of loving fellow Christians. But should a Christian teacher who denied the humanity of Jesus request aid, John wrote, "do not take him into your house or welcome him. Anyone who welcomes him shares in his wicked work."

John wrote: "Anyone who runs ahead and does not continue in the teaching of Christ does not have God; whoever continues in the teaching has both the Father and the Son" (2 John 9). The "teaching of Christ," in this context, is not the *teaching Christ taught*, but the *teaching about Christ*, specifically, that he came to earth in the flesh (vs. 7). Those who take the former view wrest the phrase from its context as a pretext for *not* doing precisely what John commanded: "love one another." Context determines meanings in Scripture and, unless God specifically notes otherwise, all interpretations are confined to the original intent of the texts from which they are taken.

3 John

In early 2008, the *Wall Street Journal* published a lengthy article entitled "Banned from Church." The tag line elaborated: "Reviving an ancient practice, churches are exposing sinners and shunning those who won't repent." The article centered on a 71-year-old woman in southwestern Michigan who was expelled from her church (and arrested for coming back) because she insisted the church follow the by-laws of its charter. The church leadership refused to follow the by-laws; when she talked about what they weren't doing to some of the other church members, she was accused of gossip. When she refused to stop, her membership was revoked.

A 6,000 member church in Nashville recently expelled 74 of its members for causing division in the church. Their offense? They wanted to see the church's financial records.

The first-century church was not immune to congregational difficulties. For the most part, church leaders countered division with a call to peace. In the Philippian congregation, Paul wrote to two leading women who, because of their personal differences, were dividing the church. He rebuked them because they were not acting like Jesus. He told the congregation to quit taking sides and to help these two women to resolve their differences.

There *were*, of course, those occasions in the first-century church when expulsion of a member (we'd probably call it shunning) was practiced. Sometimes, it involved a persistent moral failing of a member who refused to change his life (1 Corinthians 5). At other times, it involved members who misunderstood scripture and whose lifestyle brought shame on the whole congregation (2 Thessalonians 3). And at times, it involved church members who were, for whatever reason, just looking for power (Romans 16:17ff).

What struck me about the *WSJ* article was that, for the most part, all the cases they reviewed focused on power and who would wield it.

In an unnamed first-century congregation, there was just such a power struggle. A Christian named Diotrephes had, over time, become a respected church leader. He had become so powerful that he successfully forbade his church to listen to the apostle John (we are not given the reason). Anyone who did so

Diotrephes "put out of the church." Gaius, another Christian in the same congregation, was at a loss about what to do. Everyone respected Diotrephes. Gaius did as well. But Gaius also respected John. Gaius had no power and no influence. He wasn't taking sides, he just didn't know how to respond.

In 3 John, John *could* have written to him: "You need to take my side. After all, I am an Apostle." But he didn't. That would have just exacerbated the division. Instead, John encouraged him to continue to live in the Christ-like manner he'd been doing, and if he had any questions at all to refer them to another member, Demetrius, who was well spoken of "by everyone."

Jesus said: "You know that the rulers of the Gentiles lord it over them, and their high officials exercise authority over them. *Not so with you.* Instead, whoever wants to become great among you must be your servant, and whoever wants to be first must be your slave-- just as the Son of Man did not come to be served, but to serve, and to give his life as a ransom for many" (Matthew 20:25–28). Later Paul wrote: "We who are strong ought to bear with the failings of the weak and not to please ourselves. Each of us should please his neighbor for his good, to build him up. For even Christ did not please himself but, as it is written: 'The insults of those who insult you have fallen on me'" (Romans 15:1–3).

Sometimes harsh discipline must be meted out in within a family, and the family of God is no exception. But when that happens, we must be sure we've done all we can to follow these words first.

In difficult times, we all look for someone with a level head whose walk is closer to Christ's and further from the world's. Demetrius had such a walk. Someone may be looking for just such an example in you. How's *your* walk going?

Jude

Jude, another brother of Jesus, tells us that he started to write a treatise about "salvation." It would not have been a document about how to be saved, because his readers, he says, had already experienced salvation. We anticipate it would have been like one of Paul's letters, reminding his readers of the benefits of salvation and then, perhaps, the responsibilities. Instead, given the circumstances of his readers at the time, he felt that something else was more critical. The very fabric of the Christian religion was under attack so Jude urges his readers to "contend for the faith" that has been "for all time" given to the saints.

Under attack was the lordship of Jesus—the authority of Jesus to rule in our lives.

I am inclined to think that the challenge was to the seriousness of the call to discipleship; an insistence that God's grace through Jesus would excuse even the most vile behavior. Jude described it as changing "the grace of God into a license for immorality." While such a teaching would not specifically deny that "Jesus is Lord," it would implicitly undermine his lordship by saying that one doesn't have to take obedience seriously because grace will excuse disobedience.

Those who promoted such a view were present not only in the Christian church of Jude's readers, but even among her leadership (vs. 12), and Jude minces no words about the dangers of following them. Historically, he writes, God has not been shy about punishing the disobedient, whether they be angels or whole cities. When Jesus comes, with thousands upon thousands of his holy ones, he will "convict all the ungodly of all the ungodly acts they have done in the ungodly way, and all the harsh words ungodly sinners have spoken against him" (vs. 15). Remember: he is talking about Christians.

Until Jesus comes, how should Christians deal with this problem and those who promote it? *That* is the issue of Jude.

Jude insists that there is a *way* of faith that is incontrovertible. Our religion is not whatever we want it to be. God has spoken. We know what he said. We can understand it. And it is not subject to change, either with the times or with our whims. It is this way of faith Christians should focus on: What has God said he wants of us? Jude calls it building ourselves "up in the most Holy Faith." We must pray. We must "keep ourselves in God's love"— not becoming something God hates because we have become hateful. We must show mercy to those who are struggling with this faith, doing all we can to help them—"snatching them from the fire" (vss. 20–23). Barnabas never gave up on Mark. Jesus never gave up on his brothers. We must not give up on each other.

Ultimately, we must entrust our lives to God, making him the authority of our life. We must not excuse our failures with grace, but turn from failure and make grace the refuge of the penitent. That is the message of Jude.

Revelation

Does God care about us? Does He know what we are going through? Is He watching us? What does He think?

These are all questions the first readers of Revelation would have been asking. They are the same questions the readers of Zechariah were asking five hundred years earlier. Interestingly, God chose to answer the questions in both cases in much the same way.

The Revelation was a message given by God to the apostle John, the last surviving apostle at the end of the first century.

John wrote it down as instructed and sent it to seven Christian congregations in Asia Minor.

Revelation is not just a letter. It is art. It contains a message conveyed by a panorama of images designed to grab the imagination and underscore the power and grandeur of God. Jesus, the author of the message, appears as a man dressed in a robe reaching down to his feet with a golden sash around his chest. His head and hair are white like snow, his eyes like blazing fire. His feet are like bronze glowing in a furnace, and his voice sounds like a mighty rushing stream. In his right hand he holds stars and out of his mouth precedes a sword. His face shines like the sun.

Wow! That's the purpose of the signs—to get your attention.

Revelation has four parts:

The first part (1–3) is a direct address to the seven churches of Asia. To each, Jesus declares that he *does* know what is going on. He knows their situation, their troubles, and their weaknesses. In this, the most important part of the book, he gives direction for living so that, when the end comes—and the book emphasizes an end *is* coming—they will be ready.

The second (4–11), third (12–16), and fourth part (17–22) provide us with some repetition and each successive one builds on what goes before.

Chapters 4–11 and 12–16 follow the this outline:

- Both open with a magnificent scene in heaven (4–5 and 12).
- Jesus is presented as knowing that his followers are oppressed by the world and there are hints that he intends to do something about it (6, 12–13).

- Before the Lord executes judgment, however, he will try to get the world to repent by sending calamity on it. Before he does, he assures his own people that he knows them and will protect them (7, 14—both chapters mention the 144,000 who belong to God).
- The Lord sends the calamities, symbolized by the sound of trumpets (8–10) and the pouring of bowls of wrath (15–16), but the measures do not work. The wicked refuse to repent (compare 9:20–21 and 16:8–11).
- Ultimately, God brings this world to an end (11, 16), symbolized by flashes of lightening, earthquakes, peals of thunder, and hailstorms (compare 11:19 and 16:17–21).

The second (4–11) and third (12–16) sections build on one another. The second section attributes the troubles of the earth and the oppression of God's holy ones to earthly powers. But the third section reveals the power behind those powers: Satan.

The final section of Revelation (17–22) offers even more insight. The troubling political powers are those of Rome, guided by the devil. God will bring Rome down, and incarcerate Satan that he might never be able to trouble humankind any more. Those who have remained faithful to the Lord receive the rest and reward they have longed for, living in the presence of God forever.

If Revelation was an assurance to God's people that their Roman troublers would one day be destroyed by God, what relevance might it have for us who live two millennia later?

It is the same message for us: God is in control of all political powers in every age, and he holds their destiny in his hands.

Only those who are faithful until the end will transcend those powers and share in his glorious victory over them.

It's tempting to read Revelation with a view toward discovering what heaven will be like. There is, of course, a glorious description there. But the focus of heaven is not on walls of jasper, pearly gates and streets of gold. No one there ever glories in these. Instead, they glory in the lamb, the Christ, the bridegroom. As the old hymn goes:

> The Bride eyes not her garment, but her dear Bridegroom's face;
> I will not gaze at glory but on my King of grace.
> Not at the crown He giveth but on His pierced hand;
> The Lamb is all the glory of Immanuel's land.
> [Anne R. Cousin, "The Sands of Time Are Sinking," in Kenneth W. Osbeck, *101 Hymn Stories* (Grand Rapids, MI: Kregel, 1979), 257].

To be all our glory there, he must be all our glory here.